SYMB
REVELATION

FREDERICK
CARTER

IBIS PRESS
Berwick, Maine

Dedicated to Walter and Dorothea Clement

First US publication in 2003 by
Ibis Press, an imprint of Nicolas-Hays, Inc.
P. O. Box 1126
Berwick, ME 03901-1126
www.nicolashays.com

Distributed by Red Wheel/Weiser, LLC
Box 612
York Beach, ME 03901-0612
www.redwheelweiser.com

First published in a small edition by Desmond Harmsworth
Ltd., UK, under the title *The Dragon of Revelation*.

Library of Congress Cataloging-in-Publication Data available

Cover design by Daniel Brockman

Printed in the United States of America
BJ

SYMBOLS OF REVELATION

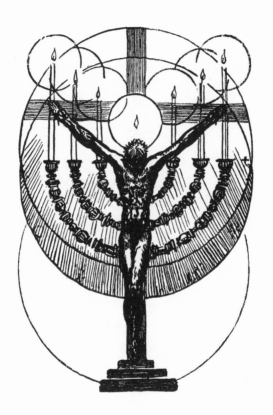

CONTENTS

A Map of the Heavens

FREDERICK CARTER

A Note by the Publisher

(From the Adam Fitzadam Edition)

A FEW months ago, in Florence, there was published a posthumous book with the title Apocalypse; its author was D. H. Lawrence and the book was issued baldly without note or foreword to explain its origin. One reviewer voiced a general complaint in saying that "there is no word with the book to enlighten us on one point of interest: the time at which Lawrence wrote it." Other statements in the same review suggested that an exact announcement as to the origin of the book was desirable and accordingly a letter appeared in the Times Literary Supplement, *July 2nd, 1931.*

The writers of the letter said: "The initial impulse came, we suggest, not from Lawrence's interest in the Apocalypse but from his interest in the theory of symbols put forward in the writings of Mr. Frederick Carter and from time to time developed by Mr. Carter in various discussions with Lawrence. In 1923, when Lawrence was in Mexico, Mr. Carter sent him a manuscript, the preliminary chapters of which were published as an introduction to The Dragon of the Alchemists *(Elkin Mathews, 1926).* Subsequently Lawrence announced his intention of taking a conspicuous part in the publication of a series of essays on the symbols in the Revelation of St. John, then in preparation by Mr. Carter, and at one time he suggested the making of a joint book.

"This latter idea held until about the end of 1929, when Lawrence told Mr. Carter that his long introductory section had already become some 20,000—30,000 words in length. Early in 1930, however, he sent the typescript of a shorter introduction that was announced by the Mandrake Press as an introduction by D. H. Lawrence to a reprint of the Revelation of St. John the Divine, *with a commentary on the symbolism and series of designs by Frederick Carter, an announcement rendered ineffective, so far as the Mandrake Press was concerned, by its closing down a short while afterwards. The Lawrence introduction was, however, without any proper reference to Mr. Carter's book, printed in the London Mercury for July, 1930, a circumstance which led to the insertion of a long letter from Mr. Carter in the September issue of that review.*

"The book under consideration by your reviewer is obviously the long first introduction to Mr. Carter's work, on which Lawrence was employed towards the end of 1929; and it is unfortunate that the publisher should have *given no clue to its derivation, especially as Mr. Middleton Murry, in his own reference in a note of acknowledgment to his recently published* Son of Woman, *is equally discreet.*

"This circumstance leads your reviewer to ascribe to Lawrence a knowledge of very many things that he derived from Mr. Carter rather than from his own 'wide reading.' Lawrence's opinions were, of course, though based on facts supplied by Mr. Carter, undeniably his own, and, indeed, though in the main coincident, yet in certain instances opposed to those of his friend. Yet it cannot be denied that Lawrence's Apocalypse *would never have been written had Lawrence not had access to Mr. Carter's work."*

An interesting letter from Mr. E. W. Titus was inserted a week later in the same review. Mr. Titus wrote: "Indirectly my bringing together the late D. H. Lawrence and Mr. Frederick Carter is responsible for the writing of the recently published Apocalypse.

"In August 1929, I had received a visit from Mr. Carter, which I had mentioned to Lawrence, to whom I had occasion to write the same day. Lawrence answered by return of post saying: 'Is Fred Carter still in Paris? If you see him tell him to send me a line.' I saw Mr. Carter again with the results that he wrote to Lawrence and visited him in November, 1929, at Bandol, Var. Lawrence wrote to me, November 20, 1929: 'Carter is here, looking a good bit older—I haven't seen him for six years. We are talking about his Apocalyptic work.'

"It would appear that Mr. Carter before visiting Lawrence had referred him by letter to some bibliographical sources, and Lawrence had asked me to procure for him in Paris L' Apocalypse de Jean, *by Alfred Loisy, and* Rituel Journalier en Egypte, *by A. Moret. From correspondence before me and my person contact with Lawrence shortly before his death (I visited him in January, 1930), the conclusion seems inevitable that* Apocalypse *is the last work from Lawrence's pen. I even venture to doubt whether he had time to finish it as planned. Under date February 3rd, he wrote me that he was about to go to a sanatorium—Ad Astra—'for a month of so.' His death occurred shortly after, as Mr. Carter strangely foretold when he had heard the institution's ominous name."*

English and American editions of Apocalypse *have both been announced and the present independent issue of Mr. Carter's work is made in the belief that it is the major document in an interesting and important collaboration.*

PREFACE

THE book recounting the final Revelation of the mysteries of a religion—the religion which has justified itself as dominating belief during a long era must contain within its compass some power outside the common order. Of the Revelation of St. John this alone is certain. Whether it is obvious in its meaning or difficult of understanding is a consideration secondary to the fact of its effective persistence. So far as this Apocalypse itself may be considered simply as a book, it reveals a strange complex of glowing images set in what is, nowadays, an admittedly confusing order.

But whether it has been fully understood or not, there is no question that its symbols have been accepted and are part of the common stock of sacerdotal figures. It is a part of the literary canon on which belief is founded and it is its last word—a final revelation.

Now symbolism in such a literature trends by virtue of its proper nature towards dramatic form. Anything less than drama or epic is too narrow and frail in structure to endure the weight and urge of an adequate system of universally significant images. The symbol in itself implies a concatenation of thought. Necessarily a vast energy must inform a work that will be able to formulate and summate thought and feeling for a new cycle of time. And this too, will be possible solely through a profound understanding of the tradition in being and the means available to its transmutation for the fresh need of the coming era.

In the New Testament certain suggestive instances of this tendency may be found, and that in the synoptic books themselves. The account of the culminating incidents verges so closely on the method of drama that, indeed, it has been put forward as being quite evidentially excerpted from an antecedent mystery play. Its affinities are undoubtedly striking. The scenes of the tragedy begin with the Last Supper and continue through the Agony in the Garden, Betrayal and Trial, to the end. But a yet more manifest example may be found in the final book, John's Revelation.

With the stage set in the heavens themselves, its properties resplendent and dazzling beyond any others in literature, its figures and apparatus more grandiose than have ever been envisaged elsewhere, the Apocalypse of St. John the Divine makes a drama transcending concurrence. Perplexing and strange though it is there can be little wonder that it gained its place in the Scriptural Canon. It is great poetry. Like the Song of Songs, another book with singular and exceptional qualities, it is a storehouse of marvellous poetic imagery and, quite obviously it is too good to be omitted. What a gap would be there without it.

It tells vividly and in astounding figures of a reintegration of all things and of the transition from one world to another in a universal regeneration. In fact it describes the way of making of a new world, expounded in the enormous forms of a cosmic ritual. It tells too, of the new day—of the new life—exalting and glorifying it in its own mystical terms; and the new period which it hailed, that perhaps never plumbed its full meaning, cherished the bright and fierce and splendid images. There is about it that fascinating extreme in dark and light which has the very glow and glory of the theatre. It gives satisfaction moreover, from simple vision to those who do not fret to comprehend by words. Psychologically there exists a curious fullness of contentment through sight; did not Job say "I have heard of thee by the hearing of the ear; but now mine eye seeth thee."

Angels are the actors in this sacred drama—angels of power, destructive, punitive, good and evil. Through apocalyptic skies move mighty and implacably fierce angels garbed in stone, and bearing vials of torments for the world. The drama there in being is the mystery play of the Universe. And its principals are the Spirit and the Soul of the World, with the ancient Dragon of manifold shapes and turns and shifts as their wicked complement. It is filled with the galloping of great horsemen, armies sweep across its scene, trumpets with world-warnings shrill ere the vials of wrath are poured, and at the last the chain and the pit await the evildoer.

But it must be remembered too, that this is a drama of the interior life although it recounts no personal reaction to common events. Instead it gives the history of a vision of universal consciousness. Within the heart stands that altar beneath which the martyrs lie, and from its abysses issue Apollyon and his horse-armies. For man—little man—is the Microcosm in whom exists in potential the very form and pattern of the great world. The great world—the universe is the Macrocosm, the vast and heavenly Man—the Adam Kadmon of Jewish mysticism. So it comes that man may seek and find within himself the very realm of heaven and, indeed, find it there only.

Searching within, descending to the very spark of his origin—the genitive plasm—he may discover the universe. In the tiny seed that makes conception lies the gate and the way there where is hidden the very star germ—from Adam's fatherhood—from Adam the protoplast. Back "before Abraham was" the seeker needs must go to find that door. He must enter in by the road of birth and death, through womb and through grave—even to that place where time no more is—rising with the last trump, ere to him the vision of the Soul of the World might adumbrate.

To such a one then, was vouchsafed sight of the mystical moon of blood and the black-shining midnight sun in the border world beyond our living kind. There he came to know the event and passing of great powers who are throned in storm cloud and thunders, angels who warn and who smite. Of this nature is the occult mysterious vision and such is the sight in darkness that discovers the unseen—Imagination . . . that magical power in Man.

Here therefore we come on some glimpse of the purport of a Revelation that tells of the final things and of the way through change and dissolution to regeneration. Last and most difficult of all the books in the Scriptural canon, for this reason was it included at the very end. It deals with ultimate things. First is the book Genesis, where that descent into mortal life is recounted which is named the Fall. At the latter end, in its appropriate place is told the way of ascent, of recovery and triumph, and the master key to the New Eden is given. This is the Book of Revelation. No mean subject in truth, and treated by no mean mind, whosoever may have been its author—that unidentified John who dreamed a great vision in Patmos Island.

He tells in the first place that he was "in the spirit" and looking on the seven candles saw a white haired one—like unto a son of man—who gave him minatory messages to the churches of adjacent cities. Then was he rapt up to heaven to see the vast stage of the cosmos where clouds are the curtains and thunders a chorus whose clangour marks the progress scene by scene. Definite, clear, with the concision of hard relief, the figures and the events of the vision have the sharp intensity of objects seen by a lightning flash. In the eye of the seer is no confusion; we it is who halt in our apprehension.

One matter suggests that a strict basis of order exists in the presentation of its events; time after time in due succession groups of seven angels appear—seven after seven the mystical number recurs—and they proceed to perform their part in a stupendous renovation of the world. Other yet mightier figures are seen in their intervals but our eyes dazzle, our ears are deafened, their messages sometimes confound our understanding. Yet withal, it is well not to forget that this drama has its own proper order and continuity, progressing triumphantly through a welter of legendary figure and ancient myth to its final climax in the Coming of the Bride to meet the Bridegroom —the eternal and the ever-recurring subject in drama or in rite.

The seer told of the way to the resolution of the problem of the Fall. His spirit sought the paths beyond the grave there to attain the eternal Woman—the infinite glory of beauty—the true Soul of the World, the first Eve. "In the spirit" he met the Angel at the gate with the flaming sword and the seven stars in his hand.

And thereafter, climbing the heavens his spirit had seen the opening of the seven sealed book of Fate, heard the Trumpets and the Thunders, and had known the new birth with the dragon looking on. He saw the cosmic reaping of corn and the treading of the vine press and forded the blood stream to the bridles of the horses. And saw then, the Scarlet Queen with the wine Cup who rides the seven headed serpent, the goddess of hucksters, shipmasters, and kings of the earth, and he saw her going up in smoke after the cups were poured. He joined in the sacred Marriage, the last of all revelations, partaking of the Tree of Life, so long forbidden, which grows in the midst of the new city. He himself—in the spirit—he had found the ultimate wonder the tower-crowned queen, he had taken her as Bride and had eaten of the Holy Tree.

The scholars in general have broken their teeth upon this Apocalypse. It has been well called "The Nightmare of the exegete." Really the book would appear to be a little too simple to be compre-hended by the expert. Its sources flow too clear to satisfy him and the poetry in it he finds to be outside his understanding. Of the mighty army of humbugs and prognosticators it need hardly be said that they have done their best to defile it. Still, its simplicity is not of the sort to be understood by every reader who scans a page. Compact and significant this book requires some degree of attention and study, surely no excessive demand in the case of a work that sets forth the mysterious, universal and secret purport of the holy ritual.

THE ANTIQUE UNIVERSE

RIGHT up to the times of the Renaissance—all through the period of history as we know it—for three thousand years or so, the world was regarded not merely as an extension of man's self but, rather was it a greater Man—it was a projection of his ego. Casting his thoughts upon the heavens he saw in its shining and in its darkness, in its system and rule, its mastery of life in year and in day, in growth and in death, that which he felt within himself as a potency and desired to bring to perfection. Thus then was the All—the Universe—a man and more than man, a divine Man. And so, man—little man—seeing himself in the skies reflected as in a looking glass, declared himself to be made in the image of God.

Living thus ensphered within the great body of power that moves so tremendously, so intently and quietly in the skies, man felt that here was the mind of the great Cosmos functioning before him. Just as within himself he fancied might live some tiny creature seeing his thoughts move silently and smoothly—seeing them as anticipating and regulating actions, and considering the future, hearing also a voice like unintelligible thunders—so then might he the lesser man himself read in the skies that which would be forth-coming later. In the stars' movements he could see the thoughts of Heaven. The Book of Fate it seemed to him, was written in the stars for the wise to read. But there is nothing of the mentality of the primitive—so-called—in this type of imaginative thought; it belonged in fact to a high level of culture in art and in living.

And not for just a little while did this go on, not simply for those few years called the Dark Ages, though indeed Dante then wrote the last great exemplar of universal epic established on that theological science. Even in his time it was aged and enfeebled and had been in decline for a thousand years.

From far-off sanctuaries its practitioners had come in the New Testament to find the newborn child—three Magi, wise men from the East, stargazers. Tradition calls them the Three Kings who sought

17

in the Royal house in Jerusalem that fourth monarch whose birth should be found under the other of the four Royal Stars. They, in the East at the time of his conception had seen the burning star Antares, the Foe of Mars, in the sky to westward. And when after journeying long months in that direction they reached Jerusalem the time of birth was come and they saw it stand before them now in the morning, to the south over Bethlehem.

And it would seem that to recount the life of the Lord Christ adequately Matthew felt the need to bring forward as witness these old astrologers, bringing them to worship and with gifts accredit the newborn master of the world. For in them was the knowledge of the World's way, its past history, its present state and that which would come. From the great city in the East, from Babylon, yet flowed the source of wisdom, and there still lived those who were most learned in the number and the way going of the stars of heaven. A Nativity would be incomplete without its Astrologer to interpret. Here were the chief of them.

And it had gone about in the world, this religion of theirs, or science as it may most conveniently be called, into all lands had it made a way. But it did not destroy the gods of the land when it came; far from that indeed, it bolstered them up. They were uplifted, made great, they crept up out of the underworld and the miry places of the dead. Man lifted his head and saw the realms of fire from which life came, and while he clapped on his crown a cap of stars, his feet were planted on the earth whence he had grown from the star seed. A mighty pride grew in him for he was well-born, a child of heaven.

But he would not forget himself in any effort he made to delimitate the bound of physical and spiritual. The earth was the centre about which all above and beneath was spinning, and the spirit was alive just as the body was alive, as part of an order arranged in regular degrees of ascent from sphere to sphere. He was Man. And the centre of interest to him was human, a necessary and natural state of mind, and so the world went on all about him for he was its measure.

Today we suffer from a certain inculcated modesty and it impedes our vision: the heavens are far off. Our wits are flooded with abstractions. We are taught that the sun does not rise. No, it is the earth that turns. We are perched on a sort of spinning top racing round a globe of fire. Very valuable information for an astronomer is this, of course, but nevertheless, despite this whirl, we in general stick to the old terms and talk of sunrise and of sunset. The complexities of mechanical ideas have no significance to our enchanted vision when dawn breaks upon the dark, but in the end they leave us at odds with our senses and their messages. Nowadays the paths of the stars in the heavens are obscured in our entangled thoughts, and so we come to look on them no more except as a drift of sparks across the sky.

But once—once, the skies were filled with great figures of legend, figures whose names have come down from far centuries. Their traditions had been handed on amongst the peoples, often worn down and altered in the changes of ages. Yet still something remains and moreover that which we have, though it is enfolded in myths and superstitions, represents the oldest unbroken inheritance we hold from the far past.

But far beyond their interest in pure knowledge—or so it would seem—the superstitions of men have led them to preserve and to maintain the things of old time. That antique science which discovered amongst the stars rumours of the fate of the world and of the greatest kingdoms beneath heaven, was at last brought down to reveal the secrets of his life to any petty fellow who could afford to pay for a horoscope. The stargazer, the magus, was too often a fortune teller and a seeker of gifts, not a royal and noble traveller bringing gold or frankincense or myrrh to greet and hail a new king. And whilst the old imperial cloak on the king's shoulders bore the figures of the stars, the globe in his hand was significant of his mystical dominion of the world, for he was initiate and divine. Yet, because heaven watched over him too, every little citizen also was anxious to be convinced of his own divinity.

Long had the notion of the heavenly display been a dominant motive in symbolism and divine imagery when at last it issued from the sanctuaries of the theologers and the god-seekers. And its chief image, its figure, was a globe banded by circles and ornamented with mighty symbolical and mysterious creatures. The imperial orb, the great world was a sphere transfixed by the pole. The pole was the axis about which span the stars called *fixed,* those which we name the constellations.

But this, the pole itself, swings about in a circle: it does not remain in the same place, it nods. Not only was it Homer who nodded, but his Zeus too. The great Æon changes, the great god loses his power. Time is done with him. Each age has its pole and its ruling divinity. Once the polar point, the star of the midst, was in Draco, the Great Dragon; before that it had been in Hercules, and it was in the constellation of the Lyre, the opposite side of this circle, just over 12,000 years ago, and it will be there again in about the same period of time.

About this axis move the great host of the stars of heaven. They form the celestial sphere. It was named the sphere of the fixed stars for, besides those fixed stars, exists also a group which they called errant, the planets. These have a different direction and rate of motion; and the path which they follow is marked among the fixed stars by the twelve signs of the Zodiac.

But the great heavenly sphere moving about the polar axis had its star groups of various figures. Firstly, there was a group in the north, the star circle of the sequence of polar centres consisting in the Lyre, Hercules, Draco, the Little Bear, Cepheus, the Swan, and then the Lyre again. To the old world's scheme the north was the divine and better place, the mountain of God. In the south was a vast waste of water. This of course, they saw in the skies and on earth: the one corresponded to the other.

And in the skies the great circle of the Zodiacal signs is set as it were a barrier, a wall, to guard the mountain of the divine throne from those monsters which creep and wallow in the outer place of darkness, monsters of the bitter seas on the edge of the world. As the place of disorder outside day and light the south was the realm of fear. There swim the many-headed Hydra, the whale Cetus, Serpens, the entangling snake and the Fishes in the star river Eridanus which plunges down to the deep of the south. Set in its place far south, the Scorpion seems to be the representative of these insects—water creatures, reptiles—amongst the Zodiacal constellations. That vast, dark, star figure, together with Sagittarius, the Man-horse, are two of the southernmost signs in the Ecliptic circle and indicate the place of its southern division by the Galactic stream.

In the middle of the stars of the north is set the great Dragon turning always about the polar axis and, besides that, in its coils is the very centre of the circle of the Zodiac. For the circle marked by the signs of the Zodiac lies askew from the general circumpolar motion of the stars; it represents a different activity, it is the track followed by those seven which were of old called planets, amongst whom the sun was esteemed the chief, their leader, ruler, King.

Although Lord of the world beneath, dispensing light and warmth, the sun is not so exact in his path as to conform with the motion of the fixed starry sphere. He is changeful. And his rising is not always amongst the same stars for, as the years pass, his position moves with that of the pole. The alteration in the place of the polar axis, its swing in a steady round, corresponds to his aberration. He is not to be depended on for a thousand years. Time moves away from him also. The constellated order of the stars continues in its path, but the sun and his companion planets seem to strive against that fixed sphere.

As seen from the earth the great body of the stars moves westward from the East. This is the simple aspect of the skies when we look on it from the earth, and, each day, the sun goes the same way, rising in the east and sinking in the west. But in the year it is apparent that the sun's motion in its circle really tends eastward, so that his path is backward—retrograde—from the stars. He moves against them and also his course is at an oblique angle to the equator.

And the pole changes because the Earth, set between sun and moon, is subject to their drawing and pulling, sometimes together, sometimes against one another. Their attractions in sum deflect her turning, so that there is a sag in her true spin and she wobbles a little.

Moreover all these things which belonged to sun and moon, months, years, seasons, eclipses and so on, all that occurs within the ecliptic circle, was attributed to the great dragon power as being the master of the way of the world. For his place is in the North, circling around as if guarding the polar axis. About that he turns incessantly whilst at the same time he himself is central and in the very middle of the Zodiacal circle of signs.

So, in the glittering heavens, there are twelve signs and, besides, a great golden dragon, Draco. About the pole, therefore, there are two turning movements, one movement of the fixed stars and one, indicated by the dragon, that of the sun, moon and five planets; for the centre of this latter, whose path is the Zodiac, lies in the folds of the Dragon.

Such then is the relation (or disassociation) of the two sets of star movements; there are those which wheel about the north pole and also those others that move with the Dragon, going on their path at an angle to the rest and at a quite different pace. In fact they draw back from the others, and though pulled by the general motion of the stars, they actually, in their own motion, travel in the opposite direction, namely from West to East.

Moreover, these planets, as stars, have quite another character from the generality of stars, for they are nearer to the Earth. They have too, a variability and eccentricity in their motions which man felt existed in his own temperament, and so he attributed to them the lordship of the significant types of character that he found in the human soul. They gave the "Humours" of mankind, Melancholic, Jovial, Mercurial, etc.

The seven planets or "wandering" stars that were seen to circle in the Ecliptic path round the earth are, in their order of apparent distance, Saturn, the furthest, then Jupiter, Mars, the Sun, Venus, Mercury and the Moon. They all had their typical parallels among the metals, as also in the days of the week, and again among the seven deadly sins, and yet again in the physical and psychological constitution of man; thus the symbol of the planet would indicate each and all of these. Of course, it is not to be forgot that these deites are the Greek attributions and only in a certain limited degree resemble the more ancient star gods of Chaldea or Sumer, of whom, as yet, we know little enough.

♄ Saturn, far-off, slow and livid as a star, amongst metals was Lead. Sloth was his vice; he was miserly, cold, malefic in disposition. His qualities in general signified old age, experience and weighty judgment and a saturnine humour. His vowel in the Greek alphabet is Ω

♃ Jupiter, a brilliant planet, shining and benevolent, stands between pale Saturn and red Mars. He is temperate, and his metal is Tin. His vice is that of strife for wealth and rule, but his disposition is genial and his significance fortunate. His vowel is Ψ

♂ Mars is red, burning, impetuous, moving rapidly, with short irregular retrogradations. War, plague and sudden death are his evil gifts to man. His metal is Iron and his significance is unfortunate; he is the "Lesser infortune" as Saturn is the greater. Violent disturbance and disorder of all sorts come from Mars. His vowel is O.

⊙ Sun, ruler and leader of all these others is imaged as garlanded or crowned. He is the divinity of all this lesser world for he is guide and charioteer in the circuit of the great road of signs that separates the lower and southern heaven from the upper divine one of the north. His increasing feebleness and lowness in the sky on the southern part of his path, as in Scorpio, is indicative of the deathly nature of that lower heaven. In Capricorn he was renewed, or reborn like a child. His nature is fiery, he is lord of the year with its life and growth, and his vice is arrogance. Gold is his metal and his vowel is I.

♀ Venus who is Lucifer and Vesper, star of morn and eve, is feminine, humid, generative. She is given the plastic metal Copper. Being always close to the Sun, she is accounted warm in her nature, and her vice is Lust and misleading beauty. With the Moon she forms the pair of feminine types in the seven planets. Her vowel is H.

☿ Mercury, who also is a servant of the Sun and stands always close to the great lightgiver, is the messenger planet, the star of the Greek Hermes who is the guide of souls, cunning, adroit in temper, but has the vice of deceit. His metal is Quicksilver and his vowel is E.

☽ Moon is the closest to Earth and with the Sun forms that pair whose influence is most manifest. Her period of time is the month, and those things feminine that go with it, much as the Sun's period is the year. She is the divinity of change and of growth and decay, a passive mirror of the sun's fecundating light. Her vowel is A.

And as these planets were seen to encircle the earth in their diverse periods, following always the Ecliptic track, they were regarded as watchers and guardians. Moreover, according to their various distances from the central Earth they were taken to be stages in a progression to and from the sphere of the fixed stars. For each planet was set as it were on the surface of a sphere whose dimension was indicated by the diameter of the planet's circular path around the earth. So the universe was taken to be like a set of bubbles, each within another, transparent spheres, all full of powers which were invisible to human eyes except as signified by the star—the planet—set in each like a jewel in the ring of its orbit.

In the ascent of the heavens the first stage was made by way of the Moon, then by Mercury and Venus to the Sun, after that by Mars and Jupiter, and, last, the throne of Saturn, the seventh gate. Once having discharged its responsibilities to these seven who had given to it the garments in which to descend into terrestrial life then the spirit might walk among the further stars of heaven.

Man had made for himself, in fact, a world which grew with root and stem and branch and leaf like a tree. As above, so below, says the Hermetic proverb. He could climb to its topmost boughs; in spirit, at least, he could fly. If in it were seven branches, then its roots were seven, at its foot flowed the stream of life. And on it hung the star clusters like fruit, and the four winds blew on it. At any rate it was all alive to him and a marvellous and fine invention; alive indeed, and the veritable tree of life. And so it reacted upon him as a living thing, a semblable. He saw himself as like it.

Not until the Mathematicians had evolved elaborate methods of calculation and checked ever more closely its motions and structure did it lose the sense of a fuller but complementary life parallel to man's own. But the invention of many devices like the Arabic numerals and such conveniences brought in pure mathematics and arid abstractions and prodigies of quantity, number and size, so that all things were pushed away far off each from each and stiffened into deathly and empty hollowness.

No more could the sun be seen "stationed in the midst wearing the cosmos as a wreath." That vision had belonged to theology as a fount of poetry. Then he was a god belonging to a great order; he was a ruler in heaven and from the days of old Chaldea, the Lion, Leo, had held his royal star. But in the process of being made efficient, the calendar's practical value had become overwhelmingly important and with that its ceremonial significance shrank. The priest lost his philosophy and succumbed into ritual forms, the philosopher lost his religious sense, his feeling for a proportionate relation interbinding earth with heaven—and he became caught up in mechanical definitions. Life became uneasy.

Yet before our watching eyes the planets still strive with the constellations, the Moon yet glows with wonder in the night. The poet that is in us all is caught into their tides of glory and mystery when by chance we look long into the bright skies. And so do many of our words still hold all the old sense of the nearness to our life of the living heaven—and the planets still rule many things in our lives.

The moon is to us even yet the great exemplar of the feminine power in the cosmos as it sways the waters of the sea in the tidal movements each day. And in the month it rules the life of woman in the manifest period of her sex.

From the moon comes also our week of seven days. This is the quarter of her period of revolution through the stars and in it each day is appointed to one of the planets and bears its name. By this it comes about that each of the moon's twenty-eight stations—the Mansions of the Moon—in the Zodiac has its recurring succession of planetary rulers: Sun, Moon, Mars, Mercury, Jupiter, Venus and Saturn— Sunday, Monday, Tuesday, Wednesday, Thursday, Friday, Saturday (nearly all these names are taken from the northern gods who were equalled with those of the Mediterranean—Freya and Venus: Woden and Mercury)—a planetary succession which was four times repeated in the month.

Earlier, the moon's path was divided into three periods of ten days, taking its time—thirty days—between conjunctions with the sun as the standard; that is to say, its times of Waxing, Fullness and Waning. In this it conformed with the similar ancient division in the sun's path who had his own royal house in Leo, the place of his Spring exaltation in Aries, and, in Sagittarius, the house of his joy in Autumn. Those ancient astrologers of Babylon had a liking for triads, for sixes and for twelves and saw them throughout the world, or three worlds as they called them. Thence indeed it would appear our circle possesses 360 degrees, and a division of the sky circle into its twelve chief parts each having three sections marked into tenths again—thirty degrees to each.

Originating from the sixfold divisions found by the radius of the circle, presumably related to this, was the long established scheme of 36 star groups or constellations standing to North and South outside the Zodiac, a total, as Ptolemy's list gives it, of 48 astral figures in the skies. The "twelve" themselves are, of course, the great path of the "errant" stars, the planets, stars that deviate from the great turning movement of the whole heavens.

And so these twelve signs are the stars that mark out the body of Man wherein is sealed his Fate by the seven. How far back in history they were distinguished, and their images devised originally, is unknown. Some of its figures have altered somewhat but, in the main, it has endured for thousands of years, making manifest the great types of life in the year's round as they were when man first found the path of the sun and matched his thought against the height of heaven.

How many times since that time the sun has changed his rising sign at the Equinox can hardly be said. Now we are near the point of change once again, this time from the Fishes to the Waterpourer. Two thousand years ago the sun left his Equinoctial sign, the Ram, and entered the Fishes. From which came without doubt the singular use of the symbol of the fish by the earlier Christians. The use of the earlier Jewish image of the slain Lamb of Passover was not adopted until later on by the Church. It was, in fact, the symbol of another age, an earlier one and as such a regression.

Perhaps the slaying and resurrection had a more complex celestial significance. Yet the sun cannot rise in that sign after his winter sleep and bring in the first day of Spring ever again for many a thousand circling years.

Before the days of the Lamb, the Bull opened the year: and before that, the Twins. In them may be signified the superhuman pair, sun and moon, who make our days and seasons here below, the great luminaries, whose inter-relation lends purport to the elaborate adjustment of the great Church festival of Easter. For Easter is the feast of the sun's triumph over darkness and not till the moon has passed her fullness and wanes is it felt that the winter of the long dark nights is over and the sun, and Spring, and day is come, for she is Lady of night as he is Lord of day. She rides high and bright in the winter skies when he hangs low and sullen and weak.

It is possible that with a kindred purport the Twins were set at this point where the Zodiacal path intersects the shining circle of the stars—the Milky Way. This is the true star circle, a vast ring of eternal light, not merely—as is the Zodiac—the track of certain stars projected into a sequence of great figures of life and its types. This Galaxy was the true road and path of the great gods and thence came, they fancied, the diviner origins of man's being.

Traditionally it was the primal light existing before the lesser stars were created and the place to which the soul returns to bliss and contemplation after life. It is the ladder of Angels or the Elysian Fields.

As we see it in the skies the Galaxy crosses the whole sky in a stream of light, like star dust sprinkled with great stars. In fact all about it are stars and their constellations and the heavens are darker and more empty at a distance from it. Thus, naturally, it seemed to be the fount of the celestially manifest star life. And thence came too the old belief of a prenatal descent into life beginning from the Galaxy and continuing by way of the Zodiac and the Planets. The soul of man coming by such a path into this world could, after he had his days of living—one life or many—return; that was agreed. In fact but for the loss of memory in the stream of forgetting he would be able to find his way about the great world at any time. It was his inheritance. He was part animal, but, in part, divine also.

About this, their world, they saw the great ring of the Galaxy, therefore, as a boundary girding and containing it above and beneath the horizon; it was a girdle of light made of the original fire from which were born the sun and moon—so they, enchanted by its splendour, thought of it. There was, too, that other girdling circle going about the world, the Zodiac. They crossed at the two signs of Gemini and Sagittarius: the former constellation is on the northerly side (or tilt) of the Ecliptic circle and the latter at the southern. For both these star circles are askew and tilted away from the polar axis and from the earth's equator. Thus the world was viewed as a great sphere banded about with certain circles and defined by symbolical images. The figures of the Twins are at the point of separation and reconciliation near the highest, the northern point of the Zodiac; Sagittarius is the grim guardian of the gate of the underworld, the double-bodied figure whose horse symbol is that of the god of the deep, Poseidon. Yet more it is the typical image of that ecstatic and triumphant ride, whether in the chariot of fire, or on winged horse, or as a horseman, that has so often been recorded as significant of the visionary recovery of the lost memory and the secret way through both hell and heaven. And this, perhaps, is indicated by the figures among the stars for a peculiarly large proportion among the constellations have the horse included in their forms. The other images most frequently repeated are human or serpentine. The typical figures in the heavens are human—man and woman—equine, and dracontic or serpentine. There is of course a part of the heavens filled by winged creatures—Aquila, Cygnus, Pegasus—and another occupied by fishes—Cetus, Pisces, Piscis—but Cetus belongs also to the monsters as Pegasus to the horses.

All the old star groups below the horizon represented figures of terror, and round about the circle of the Zodiac was a terrifying and monstrous group of great water creatures. From the urn of Aquarius runs a stream in which are fishes; beyond that is the great Cetus, a monster lying beneath Aries and Taurus and wallowing in the river Eridanus' waters which run southward and ever south. Next come the figures of the two Dogs beside the Galaxy which here crosses the Zodiac. Beneath the figures of the Crab, the Lion and the Virgin is the long Hydra.

Scorpio—the vast constellation figure of the scorpion—has its head and claws in the Ecliptic, but though a Zodiacal sign, its body, tail and sting stretch far away southwards. Standing over it in the North is the constellation called Ophiucus or Serpentarius, the man in the coils of Serpens, the snake among the stars. This serpent stretches up to the head of Draco in the North and between their two heads are the crown of the North, Corona Borealis, and the foot of Hercules, who, with his feet and knees to the Pole, has his head beside that of Ophiucus, whilst their bodies extend in opposite directions north and south.

That part of the sky is obviously distinguished by these peculiar figures, a group made up of human and reptile creatures inter-mixed, joining north and south. There is Serpentarius struggling in the snake's coils, Hercules over him upside down, with one foot on the head of Draco and the other on the Crown that is over the head of Serpens. Beside them strides Bootes the driver of the great Plough (or the warden of the Great Bear) who follows Helike—the great Plough, or Bear, or Wain—as it turns about the Pole. He was named also the bearer of the Goad or the Vine-dresser and again, the Spearman or Shouter—Clamator, the Herald.

Draco, Serpens and Scorpio, Hercules, Serpentarius and Bootes, thus are they named, these six, and they have the great stars Arcturus, Vega, and Antares among them in a triangle, Lyra, Vega's constellation, being just beside the outstretched hand of Hercules.

These star figures are paralleled in a set of constellations lying in the path of the Galaxy on the opposite horizon, Perseus the trium-phant hero bearing the Gorgon's Head with its evil star, Algol, in his hand, Auriga the Charioteer, and Orion the giant figure between the Bull and the Twins, who fights his way up from the waters of the underworld river Eridanus.

About the Galaxy northwards, moreover, is a group of which the story indicates how clearly certain of the constellations were assimilated to myth. Thus Perseus, Andromeda, Cassiopeia and Cepheus with the monster Cetus beneath are the chief constellations to north and south of the Spring signs Taurus, Aries, and Pisces. Beside Aquarius is Pegasus and the spring of water. The Chimera—represented as part lion and part goat—both of these important constellation images—brings the story of Bellerophon into the same type. Certainly some close connection existed between the life of stars and the tales of these heroes and their struggles with Fate.

In the case of the constellation over Scorpio and Libra there is shown a conflict with serpents which has affinities with the chief adventure of Hercules. But he strove also with the Lion and the Crab, in fact his twelve labours are often cited as representative of the year's round of the sun in the signs.

However an ancient monument of the Orphic cult, itself strikingly like one belonging to the cult of Mithra, provides an image syncretising all this into one terrific being called the Great Æon, originally an Iranian or Babylonian conception of the Great Figure of Time and Night. With the body and legs of a man enfolded in the coils of the serpent, he had a leonine head with flaming mouth. About his waist were set the signs of the Zodiac; in his hands were the keys and the thunderbolt or at times a staff. Resting on top of his head was the head of the serpent. He represented, in the terms of the Calendar, Autumn and its mystery, as Mithra with backward turning head slaying the bull symbolised the Spring.

Most curious of all the myths indicated among the stars is that of the Centaurs, and one ignored apparently in literature. In the south beneath the circle of aquatic monsters that girdle the Zodiac is the Altar—Ara—and beside it stands Centaurus—the great Man-horse—who there sacrifices a creature called the Wild Beast—Therion—or Leopard or Wolf. These are the most southerly of the ancient constellations. The Altar no doubt corresponds to the Earth, symbolising the centre and hearth and place of sacrifice in the deep midst of the world. Sagittarius and Centaurus both stand beside it. From this Altar the stream of the Galaxy rises on both sides towards the north like the smoke of burning.

Manifestly the immense importance of the Galaxy as chief of all constellations, the primal figure and the rim and bound of the universe, tended to give a definite scheme to these groupings, for away from its circle stars are fewer and less bright.

Beginning then with the star groups most closely associated with its track and proceeding south from the Zodiac, Sagittarius, its most remarkable figure, stands, a great man-horse, drawing a bow, with one hoof on the Southern Crown—Corona Australis. Next beside him, for the Galaxy spreads wide here, is the Scorpion, whose body stretches south so that its sting reaches the Altar and is near the second man-horse Centaurus. In one hand he holds up the sacrifice Lupus, over against the Scorpion as if he would thrust his dart through both at once.

At the heels of Centaurus is the Southern Cross, the constellation next following, and then, up towards the north, is seen the great ship Argo.

Just south of the Zodiac but north of these figures stretches the Hydra, its tail beside Scorpio and its head below Cancer and over Argo. It forms one of the great band of reptiles nearly encircling the heavens and lying almost parallel to the Milky Way—Hydra, Scorpio, Serpens, Draco.

Near the line of the equator are the two Dogs, one on each side of the Galaxy, with the star Sirius, the Dog Star, marking Canis Major. Procyon the lesser dog, stands on the Equator close beside the Crab and the head of Hydra.

In the stream of the Galaxy above these stands the constellation of the Twins and here the circle of the Ecliptic is passed in the ascent northwards. Auriga the Charioteer who carries a goat in his arms appears next. Over him is Perseus flourishing his crooked sword, and above Perseus is Cassiopeia, the throned queen. Alongside these two star groups is set that of Andromeda, the virgin chained with outspread arms.

Standing on the summit of its great arch of glittering star dust, looking downwards towards his daughter Andromeda and to the Fishes and Waterpourer beside her, is Cepheus the King of Ethiopia. Flowing down thereafter on the other side of the north the Galaxy passes through the star-birds, Cygnus the Swan, and the Eagle Altair, to divide below into separate streams as it reaches the Zodiac in the signs Sagittarius and also Scorpio.

Generally speaking a dozen constellations stand in the Galaxy or have a substantial part of their figure therein. There is the Bow of Sagittarius, the Sting of Scorpio, the Fire of the Altar, the Hooves of Centaurus, the Southern Cross, Argo, the Feet of the Twins, Auriga, the Sword-arm of Perseus, Cassiopeia's Throne, the Swan, the Eagle. Perhaps the Head and Turban of Cepheus may be included too.

Of the Twelve signs of the Zodiac it would seem that its con-stellation figures have been designed to face almost all towards a point between Cancer and Leo and away from Aquarius, the Waterpourer—the Urn Bearer. The Lion—Leo—doubtless is the centre of interest. His star Regulus is the Royal Star. He is the heart of the Zodiac and so, of course, of the Greater Man in the old attribution of the heavens to the various parts of the human body. The division is one which gives also a certain primacy to Aries, the Ram, as the head. Taurus, the Bull, equates the neck; Gemini, the arms and shoulders; Cancer, the breasts; Leo, heart and ribs; Virgo, the belly; Libra, the buttocks and *mons veneris;* Scorpio, the genitals; Sagittarius, the thighs; Capricorn, the legs and knees; Aquarius, the calves and shins; Pisces, the feet.

Such was an aspect of the matter which interested Manilius who lived just about the beginning of this present era. The heaven was still in direct physical reaction to the Man. But the more mathematical understanding of the celestial motion which had been fermenting in Greek speculations so long found its exponent and demonstrator in the Alexandrian Ptolemy.

His work of compilation and his calculations practically estab-lished the system as it was known for the next thousand years or so. He provided mathematical rules and reasons to comprehend what had been in the main before that a sacerdotal arrangement and largely empirical. From the time that the Greeks in their philoso-phising rationalized the subject, a decline from the old high wonder was inevitable. It had been an order of tremendous figures shaking vast wings in the night and bursting in rays of flame by day; it had belonged to ritual and myth and moved august in power through the ceremonial round of the year.

Ptolemy effectively set it in order with a sufficient and comprehen‑
sive reason for everything that could be seen in the star movements
and formulas to define their recurrence in the future. No more was
there any need for intercalation of months and adjustments of
festivals by observation of the relative places of sun and moon and
stars—all could be set out in advance. The matter took on a new
aspect because the old habit of personal observation had been
dominated by the utility of mathematics. But astronomy became
more burdened by judicial astrology and the calculation of nativities;
the old religious observation of the stars steadily became moribund.

Such was the change that had been implicit in the transference
of culture—in some regards its lapse—which urged on by rationali‑
zing philosophy culminated at the time of the conquest of the known
world by Alexander of Macedon. The raw West was taking over
the power and dominion. Old centres of culture crumbled into ruin
and their kind of thought, with their sort of learning, blew away like
dust. The old order and its ritual way of approach to life failed
but its vestiges endured awhile in myths. Faint hints survive in those
stories that were told in the mythology of the young and foolish
Greeks and were distorted by their uncomprehending intelligence.
They were elaborating thought of another type in a different system.

Slight suggestions we may grasp from the powerful beings sculp‑
tured by the Assyrians, and gain a glimpse of the sense of immensity
they drew from the great life in the heavens. Just this remains to
us as we go through the list that is given by Ptolemy, thinking back—
if we can pierce beyond the enfeeblement brought over by Hellenistic
culture—back into the vast burning night when their huge bulls and
horse‑men winged and flashing swung through the darkness. Then
the sun itself was second to the moon—a lesser divinity.

Forty‑eight constellations Ptolemy gives, already long established
in his day, which are first those about the North, then those nearer the
Zodiac, and both south and north of it; finally the twelve signs
themselves.

Ursa Minor	Ophiucus	Lepus	Aries
Ursa Major	Serpens	The Dog (Canis Major)	Taurus
Draco	Sagitta	Canis Minor (Procyon)	Gemini

Cepheus	Aquila	Argo	Cancer
Auriga	Delphinus	Hydra	Leo
Corona Borealis	Equuleus (the lesser horse beside Pegasus)	Crater	Virgo
The Kneeler (Hercules)	Pegasus	Corvus	Libra
Lyra	Andromeda	Centaur	Scorpio
The Bird (Cygnus)	Triangulum	The Wild Beast (Lupus)	Sagittarius
Cassiopeia	Cetus	Ara	Capricornus
Perseus	Orion	Corona Australis.	Aquarius
Bootes	The River (Eridanus)	Piscis Australis.	Pisces

A typical ancient definition of the order of the world divides it into an ascending succession of ten heavens. Such in fact, was its form as Dante drew it out of his study of the wisdom of antiquity. Topmost was the unending Ocean of a crystalline nature, the Empyrean, consisting in water mingled with fire. Beneath this lay the heaven, called sometimes Primum Mobile, which also was esteemed to be the heaven of nebulous stars invisible except as the ring of the Galaxy. This was the ninth, and beneath it stood the visible heaven of the fixed stars, the eighth, which was represented in figure by the four royal stars, or the Cherubim. Below this are the seven heavens of the planets in their order, and beneath them the four elements, a total of fourteen degrees.

10.   OCEAN WITHOUT END

9. The star-filled expanse of nebulous light — Here worship the Seraphim.

8. The Firmament — Here sing the Cherubim.

7. The seventh heaven, of Saturn. — Here stand the Celestial Thrones.

6. The sixth heaven, of Jupiter. — Here are the Celestial Dominations or Rulers.

5. The fifth heaven, of Mars. — Here are found the Celestial Virtues.

C

4. The fourth heaven, of the Sun.	Here are the Celestial Potencies or Powers.
3. The third heaven, of Venus.	Here are the Celestial Principalities.
2. The second heaven, of Mercury.	Here are the Archangels.
1. The first heaven, of the Moon.	Here are the Angels.

Fire.
Air.
Water.
Earth.

CEREMONIAL

R EMARKING upon the popularity of astronomical apocalypses about the beginning of this present era, it has been
commented by an acute and penetrating scholar that they
obviously ministered to the widespread interest shown for sacramental
cults at the same period. They set forth "the ascension which the
ritual symbolised and guaranteed."*

Now of course religious ritual has for its foundation an assertion
of the definite and definable relation between man and the universal.
Religion proceeds to define this affinity in its ceremonial and to set
forth a scheme of their coming together. Studied comparatively, this
idea appears to be based in general upon a scheme correspondent
with the divine first creation, telling in symbol of the eternal verity
expressed in the creative word of God and its bringing to birth of this
living world. And so it yet continues (in the traditions of the Western
lands at least): ever and always is repeated the divine creative act,
changing the common elements into a vital and holy existence.

Even in ancient Egypt the daily rite was a formal repetition of the

* J. A. Stewart, "Myths of Plato," p. 367.

primordial creation through the issue into manifestation of the god Amun, showing first the light kindling in the darkness, and then the great word creating the light flash and the thunder of primaeval origins. Whether performed daily, or in a year order, the recurring rite figures an everlasting renewal in creative activity, an enduring ceremonial, incessant, lest the world should fail.

And it may be predicated of almost any religious ceremony that its order and rule accords of necessity with a divine (or in other words a universal) mode of action. This undoubtedly is so if its roots grow deep in human tradition. Every rite tends in some degree to demonstrate—to unveil in symbol—the manner of divine activity in the world.

Furthermore then, the astronomical apocalypse, revealing to the rapt, ecstatic seer the secrets of the cosmos, simply shows forth the celestial power in its ordered processes. Its arrangement is, in general, based upon a scheme of seven, for seven heavens made the familiar ancient astral series of spheres. This is completed by an eighth, a fixed, heaven—a system that with slight variations lasted throughout the period between the wide dissemination of the Chaldean star-lore, some centuries before the present era, and that of the Renaissance in Europe. Such was the "scientific" system that formed the background to ceremonial and apocalypse, and upon its theory was based their common principle.

But in Stewart's comment quoted above, one exception to the usual heaven-ascending rule in apocalyptic literature is to be remarked and in this he conforms with the general opinion. It is there asserted that the Apocalypse of St. John is not astronomical "but the scene is always changing from heaven to earth, and to hell."* Astronomical, of course, in our present-day terms actually means astrological, that is to say, it refers to the science of the stars as known to Claudius Ptolemy and his predecessors.

However, this Apocalypse of St. John so far conforms with the rule in these accounts of visionary sky journeys, that it is appointed— as are so many others—with furnishings and ornaments from the temple. Indubitably the temple was the place for vision or revelation. Moreover the Hebrew temple was arranged in an order following a celestial pattern—the temple of God in heaven. The temple candlestick with its seven branches Josephus associated with the "seven

* J. A. Stewart, "Myths of Plato," p. 361.

planets," and the twelve shewbreads on the holy table with the "twelve signs" of the Zodiac.

Conformably to this the Apocalyptic candles relate with seven lamps burning before the throne of God. There is revealed an altar of incense too, a heavenly altar served by angels, and, also, there are angels that sound trumpets. And at a certain point the holy veil is opened or sundered (passed through), for the ark of the testimony is shown in the heavenly temple.

Indeed, it may fairly be asserted that this Apocalypse is a cosmic manifestation of the ritual, on the ground that it declares itself to be the revelation of a new creation. And, certainly, some adequate solution of the peculiar obscurities presented by this the final book of the canonical Scriptures is required, now that the old opinion on its purport as the prognostication of a series of events forthcoming in world history has reached its term, and no longer satisfies any but a small body of dabblers in futurity.

Research has made more clear in recent days that the Apocalypse contains a substantial proportion of Greek and Babylonian myth figures, seen no doubt through the eyes of a Jewish visionary. The story of the woman and child and the dragon can hardly be reconciled with the synoptic account of the birth of Jesus Christ. But it conforms more nearly with the myths of Leto and the birth of Apollo, or again, in some important aspects with the story of Isis and Horus, or even, in one regard, with that of the infant Dionysus who, at birth, was caught up to his divine father enthroned in heaven. Altogether, indeed, the whole book has the air of a syncresis made in the Jewish, or Judaeo-Christian interest from symbols derived at large amongst the peoples of the Eastern Mediterranean.

And again to divide the book into two parts seems to throw a certain light upon its structure. The first part ends when the Last Trump has sounded and the temple of God—the veil of the innermost holy place—is opened in heaven to show the ark. Then Chapter XII, ensuing, describes a great wonder in heaven, the mystical birth of the Messiah takes place from the goddess crowned with the twelve stars—crowned, that is to say, with the Zodiac.* The second part of the Revelation begins.

* cf.   R. H. Charles, "Commentary on the Revelation of St. John," I. p. 315/6.

The completion of the second part and of the renewing of the world comes when the Bride, as the New Jerusalem, descends from heaven as a city standing upon the starry jewels of the Zodiac.* Here appears to be a new and a higher Jerusalem—one which has the crown of the earlier divinity as a footstool. Just as the earlier described woman in the heavens had the moon at her feet, the new Bride of the Lamb stands upon the Zodiac itself. One then is beneath, the other above the Zodiacal circle.

These figures provide a most important indication of the prime significance belonging to the symbols used in the Apocalypse. They are manifestly astral images directly connected with the stars of heaven, that is to say they are astronomical but not in our day's understanding of the term. They are mighty cosmic figures, starry symbols of an earlier age, which sought the way of the gods treading skiey paths in dreams of splendour.

Hardly possible of explanation by any other reason than a division into two complementary parts, is the striking resemblance between the plagues and horrors produced by the blasts of the seven Trumpets (cap. viii et seq.) and the pouring of the seven Vials (cap. xvi): these resemblances are capital. Such a duplication of images in the first and second parts is persistent.

Now in the daily ritual of ancient Egypt† is a division into two distinct sections, one South and one of the North, the one part repeating the other in general arrangement. The same typical division may be found in the Roman Mass, where the Missal is changed from the South side—signifying the old Law—to the Gospel side, the North side of the Altar. At this part of the rite in the early days of Christianity the catechumens withdrew and only the initiated remained. The North and South symbolism represented a difference in degree at least—an outer and an inner, a beneath and an above.

In ancient astral symbolism it was the rule that the south part of the universe was the underworld of dark and night. The sun, descending below the horizon at eve, strove through its obscurity all the night-time. Light was a distinctive and separate entity, and the

* *ibid. II. p. 166/8. The Ven. Archdeacon Charles deals at length with the twelve-starred crown and with the Zodiacal symbols corresponding to the gems of the foundation.*

† *cf. A. Moret, "Rituel Journalier en Egypte."*

north was its proper place; there (for the creation of light preceded that of sun, moon and stars—Gen. i.), in the Northern hemisphere, was the upper world of day. The sun at night was in the south hemisphere, the underworld.

Around this upper world of the north heaven stands the Zodiac, with its twelve "gates" or "castles" as a wall guarding against the star-figured monsters wallowing in the under-deep of the southern abyss.* The universe consisted in two parts, one beneath and one above the circle of twelve signs.

Yet again, such a south and north division is found in the arrangement of the Candlesticks, the golden Altar of incense, and the Holy Table in the Hebrew Tabernacle. To the south side is placed the candlestick of seven branches; in the midst is the altar of incense; and the table of the twelve shewbreads of the tribes stands on the north side. These loaves or cakes are described as the "most holy unto him of the offerings of the Lord made by fire by a perpetual statute." (Lev. xxv, 9.).

Here then, may well be one source of the figurative number of stars worn by the woman appearing in the heavens, recorded by St. John (Rev. xii, 1, et seq.), for in the Apocalypse the movement, as indicated by the temple furniture, begins with the seven candles (cap. i) and proceeds northward by way of the golden altar of incense (cap. viii). Moreover in the description of the woman threatened by the seven-headed dragon the number seven seems to be set in opposition, as if antagonistic to twelve, and throughout the second half of the Apocalypse its meaning is clearly adverse—Babylonish, in fact. To the light world seven represents darkness and the stars of night—or the underworld.

In any case these numbers, we may conclude, which possess so suggestive an import in the Book of Revelation, are significantly exemplified in the temple furniture; and the movement across the tabernacle from south to north represents a change from the symbol of seven and the number of planets, to the symbol twelve and the number of signs in the Zodiac—an ascent. And, again, the woman who is revealed in vision with the moon at her feet, though crowned with the Zodiacal twelve, is nevertheless standing upon the lowest of

* cf. S. Langdon, "The Babylonian Epic of Creation," and also a planisphere for the position of Cetus, Hydra, Serpens, Lupus, etc.

the planets: for the moon was regarded as the planet nearest earth.*
But in the later and culminating vision the New Jerusalem is shown
as standing upon the Zodiac and seems to correspond in place with
the crystalline sphere of the heavens in ancient astronomy. And so
here there is perhaps a symbolical apocalyptic transmutation of the
ancient cakes of offering into the super-celestial bread—manna of
heaven, changed from mortal and corruptible to celestially incorrupt.

MYTH

THAT the problem of the Book of Revelation should so far
have escaped successful approach from the side of comparative
mythology is a matter for surprise. For so long has it outfaced
textual critics and commentators that it would seem high time for
this Apocalypse to be examined seriously from the comparative
point of view. Some advantage may be gained if it is considered
simply as a collation of myths. However much has been implied in
recent commentaries, no really full discussion of its constituent parts
has been carried out, nor, as a consequence, has any commentator
arrived at a feasible explanation of its structural order.

Regarded from such an aspect there would appear to be vastly
more material suitable to the hand of the mythographer than for the
Christian theologian. To the latter the ground is dangerously under-
mined by the peculiar incongruities of the story of the Messianic
birth (cap. xii). This, so far, has been difficult of equation with the
synoptic history. To begin with, it suggests in itself that constituent

* *Plutarch in his Roman Questions (lxxxvi) in answer to a query of
why those who are supposed to be of particularly noble birth wear crescents on
their shoes, says: It is as Kastor says an emblem of the dwelling in the moon
of which they tell us, and a promise that after death their souls shall once
have the moon beneath their feet. Elsewhere, in his essay upon "The Apparent
face in the Moon," Plutarch discussed the moon as the intermediate dwelling
place of discarnate souls.*

myths have been adapted to this work with but little manipulation or internal change and therefore that an apparent confusion is due to the association of distinctive myths without complete interfusion.

The rich field of Apocalyptic figure is indeed filled with strange stories and immemorial symbols. A treasury of an ancient far-off time lies here awaiting the digger. Viewed from one aspect, too long has it been surrounded with a queer haze of prophecy and prognostication, from another side it has been prodded and raked over to furnish scientific details of early Church history. Two schools, one historic-textual, the other prophetic-theological have occupied the ground to the exclusion of all others—or nearly all. A few writers have endeavoured at various periods and with some success, to allocate counterparts for certain of the Apocalyptic symbols amongst the constellation figures in the starry heavens.

Leaving on one side expositions made in the historical and theological interest, it may be well to consider carefully the stories contained in St. John's Revelation as a group of myths, assimilated in a certain degree to a series. When it is so divided into its constituent parts, an opinion on the structure of this Revelation may be formed without trespassing on the province of the theologian . . . .

First then, at the opening of the Book of Revelation a vision is seen—a figure standing amongst seven candlesticks—a cosmic figure with seven stars in his hand, and a voice as the sound of many waters. The Apocalyptic writer states that he is "in the spirit," and receives messages to the spirits of the seven churches who are represented by the seven lights. Now although this figurative group of candles belongs to the type of symbol which had its place in the Jewish temple as the seven-branched candlestick, another, perhaps closer, analogy may be found actually extant.

In "Mycenaean Tree and Pillar Cults," Sir Arthur Evans recounts his visit to an oracular cave frequented by the Moslems. A drawing illustrating the arrangement of this cave shows a central pillar of stone at the foot of which are set seven lighted candles, and on seeing this picture, at once the opening vision of the Apocalypse is called to mind. The use of caves as places of worship is immensely old in the East. Such a continuance of practice in the present day shows that it is not repugnant to a monotheistic theology. Caves were frequently used about the beginning of our era by the pagan peoples as temples of initiation or for the purpose of secret rites, and in Neoplatonic writings* the name itself attained a mystical significance.

A parallel image to that of the figure holding seven stars is found in the curious description from the "Greek magic papyri," of Mithra who holds the stars of the Bear in his hand.† This document reveals the purport of such a figure to be that of the cosmocrator who holds —who twirls—the pivot of the universe. The pillar with lamps burning in the Moslem cave appears further to be a derivation from the ancient Zend worship of the seven stars. Among the present-day order of Dervishes the "pivot" is a sacred title held by certain of their leaders.

All this seems to belong to a traditional and persisting current of belief about the proper arrangement of that place which is used for the reception of visions, in short, the adytum.

After the delivery of the seven oracular messages from the midst of the candles, a voice called to John, "Come up hither." A door was opened in heaven and he ascended. There he saw enthroned the white-haired ancient of days with a sealed book in his hand, and an angel proclaiming "Who is worthy to open the book?" Here the Almighty of the Old Testament is envisaged (cf. Book of Daniel) as being identical in form with the Time spirit of the Gentiles and Astro-theologers.

One by one the seals are opened. With the first four appear the familiar horsemen. But these are by no means the only symbolical horsemen to be found among the Apocalyptic figures. Two later groups of horsemen are described in Cap. ix; at the fifth and sixth trumps they come forth from the abyss with Apollyon as their King.

It has been remarked that they correspond exactly, in their form and its most characteristic detail, with certain Assyrian monuments, chiefly, in their centaur shape, and in having wings and a scorpion sting in their tails. Ordinarily these Assyrian sculptures are armed with a bow but on occasion bear a sword.‡

* cf. Porphyry, "The Cave of the Nymphs," Julian, "Hymn to the Mother of the Gods." Perhaps upon this point it is worthy of comment that there was anciently a common opinion of this lower world as a cave shut in by the roof of the sky, and the myth of the cave in Plato was but one exemplar among many.

† cf. Dieterich, "Eine Mithrasliturgie."

‡ cf. F. Boll, "Aus der Offenbarung Johannis."

Then, near the end of the Revelation appears the mighty conqueror who comes in the Last Judgment leading the hosts of heaven (cap. xix, 11⁄16). He rides on a white horse like the earliest bowman but, instead of having "given unto him a crown" and being armed with a bow, he has a sword issuing from his mouth and on his head many diadems.

From first to last, altogether seven separate appearances of horsemen are described: the first four in Cap. vi 1⁄8, after these the swarms from the abyss, Cap. ix, 7⁄8, finally the seventh horseman coming in judgment.

This vision motif can hardly avoid association with the symbolical Horsemen of Israel (2 Kings, ii, 11⁄12), and the spiritual ascent that according to later Jewish speculation was made in the mystical chariot of ecstasy, the Merkabah, drawn by fiery horses.

St. John's ascent to heaven began from, or followed on, the vision in the cave of seven. This was transformed into a corresponding celestial vision, where seven lights burned before the throne, and a seven⁄sealed book was revealed in place of the seven verbal messages. But implied in this motif (the ancient idea that the things in earth beneath are a similitude of the things in heaven above) is the concept of the Temple as duly ordered to conform with the celestial pattern of the Temple of God above (Heb. viii, 5; ix, 23). And again it is equally significant that the Temple is the place of divine revelation and of inspired vision (Is. vi).

To begin with, then, the ornaments of the Temple had their heavenly counterparts, their originals both in type and in ordering. For example the seven⁄branched candlestick was—as Josephus and others declared—the lesser image of the seven stars or planets. In the Apocalyptic heavens are the seven lights, lamps of fire burning before the throne—the seven spirits of God. Also before the throne is the sea like unto crystal, corresponding to another adornment of the Temple of Solomon's building, the great laver for purifications.

As the Holy of Holies within the Temple is approached a specific series of symbolical ornaments must be passed by. Within the first veil (that of the outer sanctuary) the seven⁄branched candle⁄stick or seven candle sticks, the sea or laver of brass, the cherubim or living creatures who decorated the curtains, the altar of incense, the table for the twelve tribes. And so in the Book of Revelation these symbols are all seen and described before the blowing of the Last Trump, when the Ark of the Testimony was revealed in the Temple of Heaven.

At this point, that which has been hidden within the second veil, within the Holy of Holies, was shown forth in heaven. The curtain, the veil of the innermost, was withdrawn. From this it would appear that the latter half of the Apocalypse referred to the more secret things of the Heavenly Temple.

Moreover in the Apocalyptic progress through the divine temple, the cosmic voices of the thunders proclaim the changes as they occur stage by stage. Each group of seven angels seems to be accompanied by voice and thunders.* Thundering as the superhuman symbol of the divine Word, or Voice of God, had considerable importance in the beliefs of the ancient theologers and mystics. In the Egyptian ritual as "ma Khroōu," the True Voice, it was the creative thunder. So too, it may be related to the Logos of the Greeks. In each instance is implied a regenerative, or, creative power. It aroused and waked to life.

Now associated with this symbol of the mystical thundering is the Talmudic story of the Messiah's birth at the time of the first destruc-tion of the Temple. He was born in the midst of a great thunderstorm and was caught up to heaven, to be safely kept there until his day of manifestation and triumph should arrive. This Jewish story offers a curiously close correspondence with the Apocalyptic account of the childbirth.† In it is a mother giving birth to a divine child, who is caught up to safety in heaven. Moreover there is, symbolically, the cloud dragon of the thunder-storm and so, naturally, the outpouring of a flood of waters to be swallowed up in the earth.‡ Of course

* cf. Caps. iv, 5—Seven Candles; vi, 1—Seven Seals; viii, 5—Seven Trumps; x, 3; xi, 19 Seven Thunders; xiv, 2—Seven Reapers; xvi, 18—Seven Vials; xix, 6—Judgments.

† cf. R. H. Charles, "Apocalypse of St. John," I, p. 308, and R. Eisler, "Symbolism of the Last Supper," Quest, vol. xiv.

‡ The Talmud of Jerusalem fables that the Messiah was born in Bethlehem on the day of the (first) destruction of the temple, but was carried away from his mother shortly afterwards by a thunderstorm. He remains in his heavenly hiding place until he comes again to be revealed by the prophet Elijah. (R. Eisler, "Symbolism of the Last Supper," Quest, vol. xiv, p. 39).

certain parts of the myth have analogies also with the story of Dionysus' thunder-wrapped premature birth from Semele, and his taking up by Hermes to be enwombed in the thigh of Zeus.*

According to Gnostic and Zoharic notions the creative spell or word or laughter was a continuous sound not to be defined by letters and at the same time was a source of rejoicing and happiness. In all probability it was a sevenfold sounding of the vowels. This theme always had a curious interest for Jewish theologers. The secret name of God—the Shemhamephoresh—gave magical creative power to the man who could articulate it. Only one who had the "true" voice could pronounce it.

Now such a magical (or re-generative) significance may belong to the words of the seven thunders, for the sealing up, the keeping secret of their voices, is commanded.†

These seven thunders act as chorus to a mighty angel arrayed in cloud and rainbow, with feet of fire, bestriding land and sea—a true thunder divinity (his earlier and O. T. prototype may be found in the pair of angels of the last chapter in the Book of Daniel, one of whom, standing upon the waters of the river, tells also of "a time, times and an half," while the other stands on the river bank). Chapters x. and xi. of which these thunders form a part, are, it would seem, an interlude in the middle of the Book of Revelation, and contains an adaptation from Zechariah wherein St. John speaks of the two prophets or witnesses awaked from the dead ascending in a cloud. This narrative is peculiarly insistent on the duplication of symbols for there are two olive trees, two candlesticks, etc. He proceeds even to mention, first, the God of the earth, before whom stand the two candles, and at the end of the chapter the God in Heaven

* *But seven thundrous laughs were the means of creation according to the late-Greek magical document called "The Eighth Book of Moses." In the Old Testament the laughter of Sarah before the birth of her child "the Gaudium Veneris" is reflected in the name of the child predicted, Isaac, and the same genetic sense of the symbol is found in the myth of Dementer's laughter at Baubo's obscene antics.*

† *An older underlying myth is here remarked upon by certain commentators, who suggest that a cycle of seven thunders similar to those of the seven vials and the seven trumpets is postulated.*

whose temple was opened at the sounding of the Last Trumpet—
two gods—a surprising statement from a Christian saint.

Now Thunders, Clouds, Trumpets are the symbols of the
revelation at Sinai when two tables of the law were delivered to
Moses which were thereafter kept in the Ark of the Testimony. They
were the veritable witnesses, the testimonies of God's compact with
Israel. The little book of double taste given to be eaten by John,
to him is sweet in the mouth but to the belly bitter.

And after this interlude there is told the story of the dragon-
threatened childbirth. This revelation of the heavenly parturition,
and the war following, ensues upon the opening of the Temple of
Heaven to show the ark of the covenant.

Moreover from this point it is to be remarked that the number
seven begins to be indicated as inferior to twelve. The crown of the
woman seen in the heavens is twelve-starred, that of the dragon is
sevenfold. Here twelve is the number of the crown of stars; later, it
becomes the number of the foundations of the New Jerusalem, the
Bride, the City descending from heaven. Both instances of this
number belong to feminine figures and, in the main, the second part
of the Apocalypse is concerned with the myth of woman—the
woman? Or three women? It is just possible that these three represent
transmutations of the same feminine principle. There is the first who
is watched by the dragon, the second who is seated upon it, the third
who is the triumphant bride—perhaps types of woman as Eve, as
Rahab, and as Mary. Interrelated with this is the description of the
Last Judgment and the final wars before and after the thousand
years of the saints' rule.

At intervals throughout the whole Apocalypse various groups of
angels appear, at first sight interpolated almost at hazard amongst the
narrative. And this has been the cause of much of the confusion which
has obscured the book. Sometimes the angels are given a group title
and are engaged in the same kind of action. Such for example are the
seven Vial-pourers and the seven Trumpeters. At another occasion
the successive appearance of the angels is given, but no common
symbol or function relates them; of such a type are the seven angels
who appear at the harvesting and vintage (cap. xiv, 6-20).

As a separate series these successive groups of seven have their
own importance and purpose, but, in the main, they are distant

from, and subordinate to, the myth. They divide the book into its series of scenes and form the accompanying chorus to the events presented by the principal figures.

That an original groundwork for the Apocalypse may be found in the book of Seven Seals has been suggested by Alfred Loisy.* Manifestly the horsemen are part of the story of the opening of the Book of Fates—the Book with Seven Seals—which is the central motif in the first vision of the worshipping congregation about the throne in heaven (cap.v) and then again in the last assembly when the Book of Life is opened (cap. xx, 12-15).

The successive recurrence of the horsemen as symbols at various points in the vision and in instances so markedly separated strongly suggests their primary importance in the myth. All the parts have the appearance of having been arranged about this central motif of the Book of the Year, a typical myth form envisaging a year which had as guardian symbols Bull slayer (i.e., Centaurus) and Bull—Sagittarius and Taurus in the Zodiac, presumably of Chaldean origin. There yet survives a Jewish belief in the inscription of the Books in heaven each New Year, beginning at the Day of Atonement.

Now, just as the vision of the candlestick forms the commencement, the vision of the birth can be taken as the central myth of the Apocalypse. But if these visions have some relation to the year and its seasons—as the symbol of the Book of Fate, or its Judaeo-Chaldean equivalent the Book of the Lots of the Year, would suggest—the various parts of the Revelation may have some order based upon this fundamental idea.

Both amongst the Chaldeans earlier, and later amongst the Jews, each New Year festival was the occasion for examination of the heavenly books. But they had different seasons for it: the Chaldean year began with the Spring Equinox, the Jewish year—despite Moses' ordinance—began ritually at the Autumn Equinox. The Apocalypse cuts the knot comfortably by referring to books at the beginning and at the end.

On looking over the calendar of the Jewish ritual year, between the harvest and the vintage are to be remarked the summer fasts in memory of the (threefold) destruction of Jerusalem. As the Jewish myth of the birth of the Messiah—which is so like that in the

* "L'Apocalypse de Jean," Paris, 1923, Intro. p. 26.

Apocalypse—seems to be quite definitely related to this disaster, it can very well be equated in the calendar with this season. So, again, the figure of the Lamb " as it were slain " can refer primarily only to the season of Passover and the Spring Equinox, whether in Jewish history or Christian.

Taking it that this much is suggestive of a general principle, then the Festival of Lights or Dedication may be equated with the vision of the Candlesticks. Notably this feast was named after Enoch who was the first of mankind to be rapt up to heaven. The Apocalypse of Enoch preceded that of John by some century or more, and it recounts the secret things of the stars, the weather, the year, and the angels of times and seasons.

The festivals indicated by such a comparison of symbols may be assimilated to a tabulation of the whole Jewish calendar and its correspondent phases in the Apocalypse.

As *First* part there is the vision of the seven candlesticks which equates with the Enoch Festival or solstitial Feast of Lights (mid-winter, *i.e.,* Christmas in our calendar), called also Dedication, from the re-sanctification of the desecrated Temple under the Maccabees. This ends with John's ascent into heaven.

Secondly: the vision of the Book with seven seals and the congregation in heaven awaiting the predestinate Lamb who shall open the seals. This equates with Passover, when the symbolical sacrifice of the Lamb traditionally was instituted to signify deliverance from Egypt. To the seer the significant figure of each seal is revealed, during which time certain trumpet blasts are blown.

Thirdly: there is a vision of a mighty figure garbed in clouds whose message is accompanied by seven secret thunders. Here St. John is described as eating the little book, for he must prophesy: then the two witnesses—prophets—ascend to heaven (anticipating the Last Trump).

These symbols, the mighty angel, the clouds and secret thunders and the little book, correspond to the feast of Pentecost, traditionally the season of the revelation upon Sinai, when among trumpet blasts and thunders and thick cloud the tables of the Law were brought down by Moses.

Fourthly: the vision of the woman and child under threat from the dragon is in the Talmudic parallel related to the fall of Jerusalem.

Both stories undoubtedly relate to the Messianic birth. At the correspondent season was held the fast for the fall of Jerusalem, about the month of July—Tammuz—between harvest and vintage times. John then tells of the sevenfold reaping and terrible vintage-treading, when the blood reached the horses' bridles.

Fifth: the pouring of seven vials (cf. Lev. xxvi, 18-24) and the symbol of the three frogs has reference probably to the destruction of the Temple (threefold). There were three destroyers, Nebuchadnezzar (B.C. 586), Antiochus Epiphanes (B.C. 169), and the Roman Titus (A.D. 70).*

Sixth: at the Last Judgment when the great rider and his heavenly armies conquer the powers of evil, the great white throne, and the opening of the books, and the Book of Life are revealed. This would therefore equate with the Day of Atonement in the calendar and the traditional opening of the year books of Fate.

Seventh: after the Judgment, the New Jerusalem descends, which, following the calendar indicated, would parallel with the time of rejoicing for the Feast of Tabernacles and so the New Year. This follows, after seven times seven phases of revelation; first the seven Candles, then the seven Seals, then the seven Trumpet blasts, then the seven secret Thunders, next the seven angels of the Reaping and Vintage, then the seven Vials poured out, finally, the seven figures of the Last Judgment.

Like Solomon's temple the New Jerusalem was shown forth in the eighth month (1. Kings, vi, 38). So ended the old year and at the season when the sacred cup was filled with the water of Siloam and poured out at the altar, the vision of the new world was seen. By tradition this libation ran down over the foundation stone of the temple upon which was inscribed the all-powerful secret name of God. Here for the Jew was the very centre of the whole world, the original navel point of creation. Under this stone and the superimposed Seal of the Name, were confined the waters beneath the world which, at the time of the Noachic flood had risen from their abyss to meet the waters above and destroy mankind and drown all the world.

This festival of Tabernacles was held to celebrate the season of Noah's deliverance, and also that of his vinous sleep which

* cf. the epithet attributed to the frogs is that of destroyers (Ps. lxxviii, 45).

occasioned the division of the races of mankind into three types, Japhetic, Shemitic and Hamitic, culminating, it would seem, in the Babel of tongues and division into nations. Their ancient wrong was to be cured by the leaves of the tree growing in the midst beneath which ran the river of the Waters of Life.

Underlying these last mystical figures, and barely hidden, are the ancient traditional symbols of the Tree and the sacred Stone and the holy spring of Waters known to the West as Ygdrasil.

Marked by these significant images was the place of manifestation of the New Creation and the Holy City of Peace and the marriage of Spirit and Soul.

THE SEVEN HORSEMEN

THE valuable researches of the late Franz Boll have set the critical understanding of St. John's Revelation upon new and much more secure ground. In his *"Offenbarung Johannis"* he gives reproductions of centaur figures taken from both Chaldean and Egyptian documents. The Egyptian one is found in the square planisphere at Denderah, an astronomical decoration which shows the planets each in its proper house in the Zodiac. Of both figures (both Egyptian and Chaldean) it is manifest that the hippo-centaur represents the bow-shooter Sagittary, the Zodiacal constellation.

This figure accounts most exactly for the details in the description of the locust armies first appearing at the fifth trump in the Apocalypse. They have human faces, hair like women's hair, crowned heads, teeth as lions' teeth, wings, horse tails with scorpion stings. Moreover they have a king, Apollyon, who is the sun as destroyer. At the next resurgence of the swarm upon the following trumpet blast, the heads of the horses are spoken of as the heads of lions, their tails are like serpents.

Now close as their general resemblance may be to Chaldean monumental figures even to the extent of many particulars, it is worthy

D

of note that the whole of the significant details in their description attach to the constellation figures found between the signs Sagittarius and Leo. These are Virgo, whose hair is marked amongst the constellations as Coma Berenicis; Leo, the Lion, of course provides the leonine attributes and is the sun's (Apollo's) own house in the Ecliptic. The serpentine Hydra extends below both these signs. The Scorpion follows then after Libra the Balance; and Sagittary, the arrow-shooting centaur is the culminating figure of the imagery.

But this bow-shooter Sagittary, the crowned man-horse, bears a lively resemblance to the leader of the four figures who appear at the opening of the sealed Book—the first rider on the white horse (cap. vi, 2).

Boll finds reasons to establish this bowman as equivalent to the sign Leo owing to his solar attributes, but largely, it would seem, because he wished to arrange these four symbols in a Zodiacal sunwise order. Yet there may well be some reason for John to give the signs in reverse of their customary year order. The fact is, flatly, that in the case of the four living creatures who announce these four horsemen he does so: "The first beast was like a lion, and the second beast like a calf, and the third beast had a face as a man, and the fourth beast was like a flying eagle." According to the traditional imagery these represent the Zodiacal signs of the four quarters of heaven. Their order is contrary to the seasons. Again Dr. R. H. Charles ("Commentary on the Revelation of St. John," II, p. 158, et seq.) in discussing the New City of God defines the significant equation of the twelve foundation gems with the Zodiac. He declares that the author must have been aware of this correspondence, and remarks on the reversal of the customary sunwise order in the list.

Finally then, it would seem that the problem of the Horse-Man as symbol goes far beyond the immediate question of attributes for the locust swarms in the two Apocalyptic Woes. Indeed it extends through the whole structure of the Book of Revelation. Its entire order is concerned with, perhaps is arranged about, a succession of visions relating to horsemen. There is the group of four so familiarly known; then appear the two locust swarms; and ultimately, at the consummation of the whole event appears a mighty rider coming in judgment. And with him appears an angel standing in the sun (cap. xix, 17-18) who calls to the fowls that fly in the midst of heaven to feast on "the flesh of kings . . . and the flesh of mighty men and the flesh of horses and of them that sit on them . . ."

That the first four horsemen are introduced by the four beasts is significant of their condition as heaven's figures. Actually the symbols of most of these riders are easy to identify. Sagittarius is clearly enough the first horseman; Scorpio is the red horseman who follows him. Libra is the rider on the black horse who bears the Scales; and Virgo, who in astronomical figure is shown with harvest sickle and sheaves, is represented by the rider upon the pale horse— Death the reaper—and Hades (Biblically the grave) follows after. Beneath Virgo in the southern heaven lies the great constellation Centaurus who sacrifices a victim at the Altar. And at the opening of the fifth seal next following we are told of the souls crying from beneath the altar.*

After the simpler form of these four, the ensuing armies of horse- men in Cap. ix have a curiously complex type. Their king is the sun god in his evil guise—Apollyon. As has been remarked, the whole of the imagery of these groups of figures belongs to the celestial symbols between Sagittarius and Leo in the Zodiac.

Such indications suggest the sun's relation to the Zodiac is at least a partial motive behind these images. In the terms of ancient astronomy the sun has a position in the three parts of the heavens marked by the trigon of fiery signs Aries, Leo and Sagittarius. This is the Babylonian tripartite division of the Zodiac, marking out the circle of the world in three parts as distinct from the four parts typified by the "living creatures" Man, Bull, Lion, and Eagle. With Sagittarius the sun rejoices, to use the old astrologers' definition: this is the last autumnal sign before winter and completes the Sun's triplicity. Leo the midsummer sign is the sun's own house; and Aries the sign of the beginning of spring is the place of the sun's "Exaltation"—his resurrection from the death of winter. Such were the three seasons of the year marked in the sun's pathway.

Each of the symbolical figures marking these points is indicated by mention of a crown. Alone of the first four horsemen the Archer is described as the recipient of a crown. But the creatures who appear at the fifth trumpet blast are crowned too, and when the last rider

* *There are two centaurs amongst the constellations, one is Sagittarius, the other Centaurus. They both stand in or beside the Milky Way.*

comes in judgment he has many diadems. In astral mythology the crown belongs to the sun who is, of course, the royal star, and in the sign Leo, his house, shines the star of kingship Regulus.

This triad of symbols, the Horseman, the Lion and the Ram, has a peculiar importance in the Apocalypse. Although the Lion of Juda is announced to open the Book of Fate, the Lamb appears to perform the opening. The Lamb in turn is proclaimed as the Bridegroom who, nevertheless, comes in the shape of the seventh great Horseman.

Manifestly in view of the widespread use of the hippocentaur as a Zodiacal constellation figure it is not necessary to assume that St. John the Theologer had merely remarked the attributes of a monument and transferred them to his imagery.   From his extensive use of astral symbols it may be presumed that he had—as other writers of Apocalypses had had (*e.g.,* Enoch)—revelation of the spiritual purport and function of the heavens and their celestial figures. He belonged to the traditional type of Apocalyptic authors, was caught up to the skies, entered the heavens by a door and saw the cosmic workings.

THE FIFTH SEAL

WHEN the seals of the Book of Fate in the Apocalypse are being opened a curious change of figure takes place at the breaking of the fifth seal. The first four seals are heralded by the four living creatures, and as each cries out, a horseman with attributes suggestive of a Zodiacal constellation appears. But the next visionary image seems of another kind. It tells of an altar beneath which are the souls in waiting who cry out, asking that their blood should be avenged. They are told to rest yet for a time. Now the series of symbols of the seals according to the Zodiac begins, obviously, with Sagittarius; next is Scorpio, then the Balance, then Virgo the reaper. These are the first four; the next, the fifth following this order, is Leo, the Lion. The fourth seal foreshadows this Limbo, for its figure is described as Death riding upon a pale horse and Hades following. This is the place of the after-death waiting until judgment.

The singular correspondence between this account of the altar and Isaiah's description of Ariel (the Lion Altar)—which, too, is associated with a sealed book that none is worthy to open—naturally arrests attention. And, further, the mystical meaning conforms in substantial measure with the peculiar purport given to the Lion symbol in pagan belief. According to this Gentile theory at that point the soul in its descent from the starry heaven dropped into oblivion. The Crater beneath the Lion of the Zodiac held the draught that brought forgetfulness of the divine world. But the Hebrew prophet too, says "and the vision of all is become unto you as the words of a book that is sealed." "Drunken" said he "but not with wine, the Lord hath poured out upon you the spirit of deep sleep" (Is. xxix, 9/10/11).*

Now Macrobius, who preserved amidst the decline of the ancient world as much of the pagan tradition as he could set down, explained that in Cancer the descending soul is still in the Galaxy, but that in Leo it is separated from the Heavenly Road of Souls. We may take it as probable that in the ascent a reverse proceeding takes place, and about here should be the place of remembrance or recollection for the soul. There are many confirmatory indications of this notion of a "fall." Persephone fell into the power of Pluto when the sun was in the sign Leo, and into the chasm of Hades fell at the same time the herd of swine of Eubouleus. Helios the sun betrayed the place of her rape to Demeter her mother just as he, as the Lion, betrayed the fall of Attis to the Mother Goddess. And, much the same thing again, in Christian Gnostic symbolism, Pistis Sophia, the world soul, was tempted to her fall by a Lion-headed Æon. In each of these instances the Helios symbol is related with the fall of a typical figure—the feminine psyche.

Isaiah's commination is directed at Jerusalem—the city of David—whose tribe Judah is symbolised by the Lion. The Apocalypse, although it says that the Lion of the tribe of Juda, the root of David, hath prevailed, yet for all that, brings in the Lamb to open the sealed book.

Now of the martyrs who cry out for vengeance from beneath this

* Also A. Jeremias, "Old Testament in Ancient East," s.v. Ariel.

altar of the fifth seal, clearly it was their blood that filled the cup of the harlot of Babylon—that cup which symbolised oblivion and again the wrath of the Lord. Therein is found oblivion in the fall and wrath in the awaking and judgment, for this is the wine of divine fury which appears so often in Biblical figure.

The significance of the Lion—the red Lion—persisted for a long period and can be traced in the terminology of the Alchemists until quite late. Zosimus, a Greek alchemist of the 4th century, described a mysterious priest's self-oblation before a cup-shaped altar wherein souls were being boiled as a purgation. And so recently as the seventeenth century the conquest or destruction or transformation of the Lion defined an important stage in the Alchemical Great Work. For mythology in general the Lion is the notable and frequent symbol of the underworld and the terrors of its passage. Amongst these figurative stories may be remarked that of the prophet Daniel who was sealed in the lion's den. Again tradition of the magical efficacy of passing beneath the altar persisted also to a comparatively recent date and certain churches yet possess beneath the altar a passage through which faithful believers may creep for their soul's advantage.

As an Apocalyptic symbol the Lion, of course, held a place of considerable importance. He was the first mentioned of the four living creatures. From his astronomical significance in ancient science some appreciation of the reason for this may be found. Leo as chief—"Regulus"—of the four "fixed" signs was one of the figures of the quarters of the world. As the house of the sun this sign was also one of the fiery triad of Zodiacal signs dividing the heavens into three parts—Sagittarius where the sun "joys" and Aries where the sun is "exalted" being the two others. Leo is therefore the great point of transition in the sun's year.

Now the constellation figures mentioned already comprise a good proportion of the astronomical images used in the book of Revelation. In chief these symbols are Horseman, Lion, Lamb, and Dragon; and further, characteristic features of the Lion and the Lamb respectively are given as attributes to the two Beasts. Astronomically there was of old an intimate relation between Sagittary, the Bowman, and Draco, the central Dragon constellation, for in Sagittary was the place of "exaltation" of the Dragon's tail and the "fall" of its head. In other terms, this sign was one of the two points in the Ecliptic fixed as nodes of the moon; the second was Gemini, its opposite in the circle.

When the Apocalypse tells that the great red Dragon draws down a third of the stars of heaven with his tail (cap. xii) there seems reason in consequence to associate this with the division of the sky of stars into three parts by the three fiery Signs of the sun. When again the characteristic forms given to the first Beast (cap. xiii) suggest that its heads indicate three constellations Bear, Lion, and Pard (Ursa Major, Leo, and Lupus), examination of the planisphere shows these three star groups to divide the sphere of the heavens from far North to far South of the sign Leo. Furthermore, beneath Leo lies the many headed monster Hydra, and confirming this attribution, it possesses in myth—like the Apocalyptic creature—the curious quality of recovering from all wounds to its heads, however deadly. With this monster Hercules fought.

According to Ptolemy the following constellations or parts thereof rise in the third decan of Leo: "The neck of the Great Bear and his left hind paw, further the head and foreclaw of the Lion, the neck of the Water snake and the middle of the Ship."—(cf. Abu Mazar in Boll's "Sphaera"). Of the characteristics attributed to the first beast rising from the sea in the Apocalypse, three of these give a good general correspondence, and the Leopard (alternatively named Wolf, also called Therion, a name given to Cetus too), is the creature offered as sacrifice by the centaur at the Altar in the heavens and to the south of the constellation Argo, the Ship. In Daniel vii, 2-8, the original type of this creature is described where, equally, it appears as a sequence of attributes to the Lion sign. Daniel first describes the Lion and gives to him the part of the human frame ruled by that sign, the heart of man. His fourth beast is the tenhorned creature who is, no doubt, Hydra, at whose tail end is found the constellation of that Leopard which is being sacrificed at the Altar in the South.

Then again the other Beast (cap. xiii, 11, et seq.)which arises from the Earth is horned like a lamb. Here is another figure from the triplicity of the sun—from Aries in this instance. One of the sub-ordinate groups of stars about this sign is the head of Medusa (Algol —the Ghoul) wounded to death by the sword of Perseus. Manifestly the author's intention must be to suggest a diabolical similitude of the Lamb even to the deathly wound from which it does not die. In fact it seems to deal with an evil imitation of higher things, for in the next chapter the Lamb himself appears with the host of saints on Mount Zion. These nefarious figures are no doubt manifestations of that power which the Gnostics call the Counterfeit Spirit.

A triplicity of qualities in the great world has its correspondences in figure throughout the Bible. It derives from the antique Babylonian division of the universe into Heaven and Earth and Water, that which in the earlier books of Scripture is "Heaven above the Earth beneath and the Water under the earth" (Ex. xx, 6). The Apocalypse uses the same terms "neither in heaven, nor in earth, neither under the earth" (Rev.v, 13). In short their world was divided into heaven, earth and sea, and the sea was the underworld, the place of the dead. Monsters of the dragon—serpent—leviathan kind lived in the sea and were typical of its nature, as may be found from the star maps of antiquity. There, beneath the Ecliptic, lay the constellations of that great encircling ocean which was presumed to surround the earth, even from Sumerian times. Its borders seem to have been typified by the circle of the Zodiac whose signs were the towers of defence to the higher world.

Pursuing the analogy of a tripartite sequence, the writer has given three evil creatures as types (he defines their relationship in cap. xvi, 13, Dragon, Beast, and False Prophet). They appear as the Dragon in heaven which is anciently associated with Sagittarius as Draco the great monster in the North; then the Beast out of the sea which appears to have the characteristics of Hydra the constellation extending beneath Leo; and the False Prophet, the Beast rising out of the earth, having the two horns of a lamb. This is a constellation adjacent to Aries—most probably Cetus, which lies beneath it. These monsters are each related intimately with the three houses of the sun.

There are other salient examples of a tripartite division of qualities: for example, the great city falls in three parts just as, earlier, the Trumpets had destroyed a third part of the earth, sea, sun and moon, etc., and the dragon's tail too draws down a third part of the stars. The title of God of course, is triple: "Was and Is and Shall Be."

When the Woman in Scarlet is revealed (cap. xvii) as seated on a seven-headed dragon figure, there appears to be so little essential difference between this and the first dragon that it would seem at first sight reasonable to assume that she sits on the same creature. But the planisphere when examined shows that just south of the Ecliptic there is to be found a belt of serpentine monsters or similar vast and horrifying creatures: Serpens lies by Sagittarius (north of which again is Draco), Hydra beneath Leo, and Cetus beneath Aries. It is suggestive too, that the Woman is seated; for the first vision of a woman bearing a child stands, and she is usually associated with the constellation Virgo, Hydra stretching so far as to be beneath her in the heavens. But above Cetus sits the figure of the throned queen Cassiopeia.

Now as to the monster on which the harlot Babylon is seated, we have definite knowledge that the stars that represent their city, according to the Babylonians themselves, were Aries and Cetus.* This Scarlet Woman bears the enigmatic symbol of the cup, and upon her forehead is written Mystery. Filled with the blood of the saints the significance of this cup is manifestly evil, it is the cup of ill dreams and corporeal enchantments, the cup containing the dragon in St. John's iconographic presentment in the Middle Ages. Biblically, the symbol of the cup is generally dominated by the terms of Proverbs (cap. xxiii, 31-33) where the wine in the cup shows the serpent at the last and its draught reveals the wanton woman.

The New Testament brought in another significance, for Christ turned the water to wine and made the new age in the world, sanctifying the transmutation.

In symbol of course, Wine is the surrogate for Blood, and the Apocalypse shows the old interchangeability of the terms. When the wine-press is trodden after the reaping of the vine of the earth the blood therefrom reached to the horses' bridles.

Now blood may be considered as one of the most obscure and perhaps also one of the most significant symbols in the book of Revelation. It imposes itself on the reader in the end because of the strangely various associations that are implied in its use. So remarkable are the passages in which it occurs and, at times, so motiveless seem the episodes, that they arouse curiosity about their real and final purport.

Amongst the chief of these is the changing of the waters, streams, fountains and seas into blood. The moon too, mistress of the waters, is turned to blood when the sun is blackened: the winepress of the

*cf. S. Langdon, Intro. to "The Babylonian Epic of Creation," p. 16.

vine of the Earth runs blood. Babylon is found to be filled with blood; she was drunken with the blood of all them that were slain. The angel of the waters declares the Lord's righteousness in transforming the fountains and rivers into blood and in giving "the cup of the wine of the fierceness of his wrath," which consists in giving them "blood to drink."

The City Goddess of Babel is a strange figure suggesting death in life—the meretrix, buyer and seller, the divinity of trader and chafferer, the evil of the city incarnate living upon the blood of the world—a vampire.

We are faced in her description with queer reminders of an ancient superstition which is older than Homer. Fundamentally it associates with the primitive idea that the blood is the life. The ghost summoned from the next world—as Odysseus performed the rite—must be enticed with fresh blood. A shade, an *eidolon,* it is a mere tenuous shape except as new shed blood offers it substance and force. It drew life, a being, from the sanguinary effusion of the sacrifice. This too is allied with the old belief that no building might stand and endure unless it had been established and consecrated by the effusion of blood. Life must be given to it. Hence for the stability of the world was the Lamb slain at its foundation. His was the life blood of the living world, whence it comes that salvation is found thereby.

An opinion conforming with this notion—an opinion which lasted until recent times, holds that the human constitution consists in a soul which is thinking and formative, and besides that a separate life—the cause of motion which resides in the blood. That is to say, to use more general terms, the one is the principle of form and the other of energy. Commonly the first is figured as feminine and the latter—having a correspondent masculine trend—is the male force of the blood; in fact one is knowledge the other is life.

Here we find the old, old complementaries which were defined in the myth of the Garden of Eden. There were two trees, the tree of the Knowledge of Good and Evil and the tree of Life, and there too was the triad, Adam the male, the first living creature, Eve who budded from his side, and the Old Serpent. The mystery of the Woman and Dragon began there in Genesis, and its resolution is attained in the Apocalyptic vision when the leaves of the Tree of Life bring healing to the nations. When the dragon has been conquered and the soul of all the world is at one with the Spirit then the hierogamy is consummated. Here in the Apocalypse the Tree is double, for it grows on both sides of the River of Life.

Manifestly Eve's tree is that of Knowledge and she gave of its fruit to the man. To Adam, the male, belonged the tree of Life. Hers then was psychic, the soul, thinking shaping and potential; his was the dark energy burning in the blood.

Indeed, the first created man, the true Adam, is in name "the Red," and according to the Kabbalistic interpretation of the myth, is two-sexed, proto-plasmic; moreover they say he still dreams in that sleep which was cast on him ere he fell into division. With this problem of Soul and Spirit—for such is the proper distinction between these two human characteristics despite long confusion in the use of the terms—with this problem of *anima* and *animus* seems to be bound up an ancient theoretic notion of sexual complementaries. In each human being are both father and mother, male and female.

Female then is the human formative quality—the Soul; and male is the urge in the blood—the Spirit. And what then is the conclusion of the Apocalypse but the marriage of these—the Spirit and the Bride—at the Tree beside the running Water of Life from the great fountain in the New City. Gone was the evil city which had drunk the blood as a meretrix queen slaying to her delight, for in her had been war between soul and blood—between the woman and the spirit. As a great drama the whole book unfolds the immense ceremonial. The spirit in darkling conflict strives through many transformations. It gained unity and illumination at the vision of the seven candles—stars (planets)—in the first Mystery. Next in the Mystery of the seven thunders when time and waiting is ended and at the seventh trumpet the dead arise—then the New Child is born from the woman in the heavens and is caught up to the throne. The third mystery is the Scarlet Woman seated on the Dragon, and this is the mystery of Judgment. For as soon as the evil woman is destroyed or disappears—when her city is cast into the sea and divides into three parts—then the great rider on the white horse comes and with him the opening of the book of Life. Thereupon is announced the Bride of the Lamb whose Groom is the great Horseman.

Even in pagan symbols the principles which these two represent may be identified. We know them as Demeter and Dionysos in the mysteries of Eleusis. They are divinities of the semantic powers—or as St. Augustine puts it, of seeds dry and wet. The goddess of the Greeks, unlike the Eve of Jewry, was honoured for her discovery of the principle of fruitfulness and the means of labouring the earth, although for her it brought the loss of Persephone her daughter. However, in this goddess and the god we find the mystical apposition of corn, that is of bread, and the grape, that is to say Wine—the draught of life, the grape's blood perhaps—perhaps even it may be that corn is the fruit of knowledge and the vine of the tree of life . . . " I am the true Vine."

THE SIGN OF MYSTERY

ANCIENT Babylon, as Dr. S. Langdon has made clear in his translation of the "Babylonian Epic of Creation," was esteemed to be established in the "patterns of the constellations Aries and Cetus" by its priests and learned men. And further describing the celestial stations appointed to the great gods he explains that in Babylonian astronomy Aries is the "Sign of Mystery" of the sun which also agrees with the Greek "Hypsoma of the Sun," that is to say its "Exaltation" (Op. cit. p. 150). He then continues: "it may be assumed that the Babylonian system was the source of all the ancient theories of exaltations, signs of mystery, or in Arabic the sarafûn, top." This means "the station in which the planet was most powerful with respect to divination."

In the circle of the Zodiac the sign opposed to Aries is Libra the "sign of Mystery" of Saturn, the whitehaired aged man of astrological symbol who, says Diodorus, was called by the Chaldeans "the sun of the night" because of his importance in divination.

Now in the Apocalypse the term "mystery" is applied to three events. First to the vision of the seven candlesticks and the seven stars. Next on the occasion of the oath of the great angel who had his right foot on the sea his left on the earth and whose voice was accom⁄

panied by seven thunders. He declared that there should be Time no longer and that at the seventh trumpet the mystery of God should be finished (cap. x., 6/7). In the third instance the woman seated on a scarlet coloured beast had written on her forehead "Mystery, Babylon the Great. The mother of harlots and abominations of the earth."

Of course, the word mystery has as meaning not so much the significance of something hidden but of something revealed in figure and image—a similar purport to the word symbol.*

The first vision, that of the seven candles and the seven stars, is not confined to the delivery of messages to the churches but it is carried forward into heaven. The white haired being who appears to John enthroned in the midst is the lord of the planets—Time—who in the old astrological designs sits in judgment with the balances in one hand and the book of fate in the other. As to the seven lampstands they are the seven planets who are given seven Greek vowels Alpha to Omega as symbols (A—Moon, H—Sun, Ω—Saturn, etc.). Here the Lamb appears as Saviour opening the book of seven seals.

Deriving from the ancient astrological belief that the soul of man in its fall from and through the heavens came under the bondage of the seven guardians or watchers (the planets) the book of fate had seven seals. They set upon the soul their seven qualities or psychological tendencies which each in a greater or less degree informed its character in life. Venus for example, gave Desire—Libido; Saturn gave endurance and slow greed, and so forth. "In the Spirit" however, man was free of these bonds; when once released he sought his proper unity. If other newer terms are found preferable let it be said that the Unconscious finds itself liberated from the Censor—the Accuser.

At the middle of the book the cloud-encompassed figure whose voice is accompanied by seven thunders announces the end of Time. Between Aries and Libra a space comprising seven signs, that is to say, between the sun's sign of mystery and that of Saturn, is placed the sign of mystery of Jupiter—the ruler of the thunders—in the Zodiacal sign Cancer. In Greek myth too, he ended the rule of Saturn the Father—Time.

* By an ancient mystery people used to understand something enacted in secret, and probably offensive. To the word mystery we now attach a perfectly definite meaning. A mystery is a rite, a δρωμενον enacted with magical intent. J. E. Harrison, "Themis," 1912, p. 35.

In the latter half of the Apocalypse of the three feminine figures described two are clearly constellations. The woman in travail threatened by the dragon has been very generally and properly taken as Virgo. Babylon, the second woman, is throned upon Cetus, and not far from this constellation is Cassiopeia, the only seated woman's figure amongst the stars. In the myth of Perseus, she is the evil queen.

Standing on the sign Pisces the Fishes is the third and last of the female figures amongst the constellations—Andromeda. In this as in all other instances in the Apocalypse the order of the symbols is in reverse of the sun's year movement. The four living creatures began with Leo, Taurus and Aquarius and the Eagle follow. Similarly the first horseman appeared as Sagittarius, Scorpio, Libra and Virgo coming after.

The mystery of Babylon is the mystery of the Last Judgment and it has some definite concern with the sign Aries in so far as inter-pretation depends upon the asterisms and their order. Now the twelve foundations of the New City of Jerusalem which displaces it are the twelve jewels in the breastplate of the High Priest which had both a tribal and sidereal purport. According to Herodotus the old Babylon was built in the shape of a square, and he gave its measure, although it was not indeed so large as the New Jerusalem of John. Yet the twelve foundations of the Queen city had in part their purpose to distinguish the new from the old, for the lower one, Babylon, had seven as her typical number.

Although the foundations of the new city correspond with the ancient attributions for the Zodiacal jewels it is arranged in reverse of the sun's customary order of going. Moreover primacy and a pre-dominant emphasis is given to the jewel jasper, which equates with Pisces. "The building of the wall of it was jasper": "her light was like a jasper stone."

As the two constellations Aries and Pisces are respectively the sun's equinoctial signs in two great time periods—the first that preceding the Christian era, and the second that of the era itself—they may indicate a reason for the reversal of the accustomed sequence of the Zodiac. Pisces, which is jasper, represents the new spring sign in this fresh era of the world's life; Aries, the Ram was that of the period then past. Slowly through its Great Year, sign by sign wheels the sun, going back at the end of time to its point of departure in the great wheel of return. Astronomers knew this long before the days of St. John and the "magi" of Babylon had established their city's celestial figure at the "mystery point" of the sun in Aries.

We find then in the Apocalypse a movement in two kinds: one is by way of the calendar of festivals and the other is the sun's great return. The feasts and fasts of the year are translated into terms of the world's history to the higher, further, order of the sun's going. Traditionally, the "widdershins" movement is the way of the dead of the after life. It was in the paths of the after-life that John was going, in the way of the gods which is death to man. For we die their life and we live their death—the Divine Passion means death, a death which is eternal Life. His Revelation has its climax therefore in the celebration of the sacred Equinox when the celestial hierogamy takes place. The divine marriage of the Lamb (slain yet alive for evermore) and his Bride then takes place. This is the consummating mystery of divine wedlock at the great vernal conjunction the holy instant of renewal of the world's youth. Spirit and Soul are at one.

EXALTATION

IN view of the definite tradition of a relationship between the precious stones and the 12 signs there is a perfectly clear significance to be associated with the symbols appointed to the judge who sits on the throne with the book having seven seals in his hand (cap. iv and v). He appears "like a jasper and a sardine stone" and these two jewels are equivalent to the constellations Pisces—Jasper, and Libra—Sardius. He prefigures therefore the New City whose predominant and characteristic jewel is Pisces which is not only one of the 12 foundations but the wall thereof also.* About his throne there is

*Each of the twelve precious stones in our text is connected respectively with one of the twelve signs of the Zodiac on Egyptian and Arabian monuments. That this connection was already recognized by the Jews we learn from

moreover a rainbow of the colour of emerald, the jewel of Sagit-tarius; and this figure of the Bow-shooter is the first of the four horsemen appearing in cap. vi when the first seal of this seven sealed Book of Fate is opened.

Enthroned living for ever and ever and bearing the Book of Destinies in his hand, this figure is the typical presentment of the ancient astrological god of Time—Saturn, who has the sign Libra as his exaltation; which is according to Chaldean terminology, his "sign of mystery." From this may be derived a curious train of ideas, for just as Libra is the sign of mystery of Saturn, Pisces is the sign of mystery of Venus, the exalted Aphrodite.

Taking these two as the beginning and end of a series, with Libra as the south and depth, and Pisces in the north and height, the exaltations in the intermediate signs may be examined according to the order indicated by the series of foundations and in parallel with the groups of seven angels. Saturn with the book of seven seals corresponds with the seven messages to the Churches. Next in this order is Virgo in which sign is exalted Mercury—Hermes—the "hermetic" revealer of hidden things and guide of souls in the next world, according to classical tradition. By his very name he is the god of seals and secret things.

In the next sign, Leo, the house of the sun, there is no exaltation. It equates with the seven angels of the Trumpets. Then in Cancer following is the exaltation of Jupiter—Jupiter Tonans. Here is the place of the seven Thunders. Next, Gemini is the sign wherein occurs the exaltation of the Dragon's Head, the point of the moon's

the express statements of Philo and Josephus. The following table (from Kircher) gives the connections between the signs and the precious stones.

1. The Ram—the amethyst.	*7. The Balance—the sardius.*
2. The Bull—the hyacinth.	*8. The Scorpion—the sardonyx.*
3. The Twins—the chrysoprase.	*9. The Archer—the smaragdus.*
4. The Crab—the topaz.	*10. The Goat—the chalcedon.*
5. The Lion—the beryl.	*11. The Water-carrier—the sapphire.*
6. The Virgin—the chrysolite.	*12. The Fishes—the jasper.*

(Kircher, Oedipus Aegyptiacus).

The signs or constellations are given in a certain order, and that exactly the reverse order of the actual path of the sun through the signs.—R. H. Charles, D.D., on "The Revelation of St. John," vol. ii, p. 167.

ecliptic crossing, which is related with the group of angels who reap
the corn and the vine of the earth. Preceding this are discussed the
two beasts, one arising from the sea, the other from the earth. One of
the Twins, it may be remarked, stands in the stream of the Milky Way
and the other on its shore. Ptolemy's account of the exaltation gives
this also as the point of the "fall" of the Dragon's Tail, and in the
Apocalypse it is noteworthy that at this point it is mentioned that the
Dragon's tail casts down a third part of the stars of heaven, quite
clearly showing his stellar significance.

At the next and sixth stage, when the seven Vials are poured out,
appears the sign of the Bull where the moon is exalted. Seventh is
the sun's exaltation in Aries and the Last Judgment when the great
white horseman's appearance is hailed by an angel standing in the sun.

Finally and eighth appears the vision of a jasper city standing
upon the 12 signs or jewels—Pisces where Venus is exalted—the
divine Uranian goddess—the New Jerusalem.

THE DRAGON

O F the Dragon who is the third in the great mystical drama of
both Fall and Apotheosis we find a glittering image in midheaven. There it encoils the polar centre of the ecliptic circle.
Just as the circle of the equator has its pole among the stars of the
Lesser Bear, so the circle of the Zodiac—the Ecliptic—which is
inclined at an angle to the horizon, has its pivotal point too, and this
point is in the coils of the Dragon.

In view of the old belief that the planets are at enmity with the
fixed stars and were created by the Evil One to be inimical to the
power of the starry signs, it would therefore seem that their variable
and serpentine motion gives a significance to their association with
Draco in whose convolutions are reproduced their mazy movement.

Himself midmost of all and enfolding the unchanging pole of the
Ecliptic about which in a slow circle the pole of the Equator revolves

E

through the Great Year, the Dragon naturally was called the first created being by the Chaldean theologers. He is the all-seer, the crooked one and the accuser who seems to sway the heavens whilst encoiling the one fixed centre therein. Whatever is of nightly dark-ness is overseen by him, and so, equally, with season and change in the year, for the circle of the sun's path centres in the Dragon's coils. So then, to him are due all those irregularities in heaven and vagaries in time coming from the erring planets, all that which causes defect in man's judgment and sets him at odds with his years and his days. He it is, according to the Acts of Thomas, who is father of all reptiles and of that one who entered through the fence into Paradise and spoke with Eve. "He it is that smote the four brethren which stood upright: that sitteth on a throne over all the earth and receives back his own from them that borrow:—kin to him that is outside the ocean whose tail is in his own mouth."

The Dragon's seven heads in St. John's Apocalypse confirm his astral significance as, of course, does the description of his tail drawing down a third part of the stars. St. John's mystical account of the Dragon would then appear to be concerned with the seven powers who in astral figure set their seal on the soul in its descent from the starry realms of its preconception. In its rebirth these are the accusers and seven is their number. And the one who rules them, the Dragon—Draco—the thirteenth amongst the great signs, is the centre of the knotted circle of the intertwined paths taken by the planets in the Ecliptic. He is the maker of eclipses, the disturber of regularity and order. Yet is it not he by and through whom man gains admittance to the topmost heaven?

THE NUMBER OF THE NAME

PROBABLY the most discussed of the many problems posed by the writer of the Apocalypse is the Number of the Beast—six hundred three score and six. Despite the long enquiry of commentators it is almost certain that the clue was given by one of the earliest of their company, for Irenaeus explained it to equate with the number of a name of the sun—TEITAN. Moreover this view is supported by the old astrologers' magic sigil of the sun, a square containing six subsidiary squares wherein are arranged the numerals 1-36 in such order that each line whether counted horizontally or vertically amounts to 111 as do also the two diagonals. By simple addition furthermore the sum of the numbers 1-36 amounts to 666.

One other theologian at least has made a valuable contribution towards elucidating this perplexing figure of the Beast, for, following the statement of his author as literally as he could, BishopWordsworth in his commentary observes that the number of times the word THERION—Beast—is employed in the Book of Revelation amounts to 37, in which he is confirmed by the Concordances.

Now 37 is the characteristic prime number of 111 and possesses the curious quality that when multiplied by 3—or multiples of this number up to its cube—it produces a similar triadic figure, viz. 37 times 3=111, 37 times 6=222 and so forth. This peculiarity amongst other devices in image and number, possessed a considerable fascination for mystical and cabalistic students about the beginning of our era.

They also by a method known as Gematria read the significant number of a word. There was nothing out of the way or strange in this for at that time and until the present system of Arabic numerals was introduced the characters of the alphabet performed double duty, acting as numbers as well as letters. In the Milesian system of the Greeks, A=1 and the Great Ω=800 with intermediary values between them. A remarkable type of cross reference derived from this by which the number established the precise significance of a phrase or a name, though the strangeness really began when notions in mathematics or geometry were applied to words and sentences.

Certainly the number 666 had a significance outside Christian ideas but the system of which it was a part indubitably indicated for them names of power and divine titles in their devotional writings, even although its origins were deep set in pagan cosmical theories.

In his handbook upon the Cabala in the Greek Gnostic books, Dr. Lea draws particular attention to the number 37 on which he remarks that its multiples are used with singular frequency in the sacred books for divine names, epithets, etc., "exhibiting peculiarities for which the doctrine of chance cannot wholly account." Upon 666 he comments that "it is not emblematic of Christ in our scriptures but originally appertained to the solar divinity in the Greek 'Ο ΣΕΡΑΠΙΕ and TEITAN as in the Hebrew, Sorath and Shemesh-Jahveh=the sun of Jahveh. (The Cabala contained in the Coptic Gnostic Books, Bond and Lea, 1917, p. 66).*

Manifestly therefore, this number properly belongs to the sun and represents in some fashion a cosmic proportion, and indeed certainly it is one of a sequence of solar indices beginning with 111 or possibly with 37, the prime number. Divine titles and names were often equated with year numbers because of the vast importance of the adjustment of true time in the establishment of an ordered civilisation. When these matters were in the hands of a learned priesthood no distinction existed between sacred and profane knowledge. Astronomy was the science of divine things, the ways of God were read in the stars of heaven, and times and seasons were his appointed manifestations. So it came that ΜΕΙΘΡΑΣ, a sacred name of the Persian god=365 like the Graeco-Egyptian ABRAXAS.

If the sun in the sign Aries is taken to equate the Apocalyptic 666—for this Beast had the horns of a ram and, moreover, because near the point of the sun's exaltation stands the malefic star Algol—then it suggests itself that each of the signs of the Zodiac might be taken to equate one of these triadic numerals. The number 111 divides naturally into three parts of 37 each. A division into triads had been made by the Chaldeans for each of the twelve signs. And these third parts, of 10 degrees each, were designated decans. Each

* *It is a conclusion now accepted by many conservative scholars that a true interpretation of the "Beast" of the Apocalypse is that the Emperor Nero was the man aimed at, for his name in Hebrew NRVN = QSR (Nerun Qaisar) enumerates at 666, whilst oddly enough, if the Roman spelling "Caesar" be followed, the Greek gives as NEPΩN KAEΣAP=1332= 666+666. According to the tradition of the church, the date of the writing of the Apocalypse of St. John is about 95 A.D. But the idea of the "beast" and his number may well be older than this. The Rabbis called the Roman Language the "Roman Beast"=ROMIITH (RYMIITh+200+6+40 +10+10+400=666) thus consciously equating it with the solar power under the name Sorath (SVRTh=60+6+200+400).*

(The Apostolic Gnosis, Lea and Bond, 1919, p. 44.)

decan equates therefore with 37. Every decan was ruled by one of the 36 constellations external to the Zodiac, that is to say those north or south of the Ecliptic. The Egyptians on their part gave to each of these divisions a separate god.

But most significant of this number 37 is the intimate relationship it bears to 36—essentially the cosmic number. Even today the square of six is the basis of the division of the circle whose degrees are 360. But unfortunately the simple multiple of 6 has the defect of omitting the five days beyond the round number of the year. Yet ancient tradition and convenience have held us to the use of this sexagenary figure. Now as 36 is too small a number to represent the year without fraction, 37 used alternatively would exactly compensate or nearly enough for practical purposes. The sun's passage round the circle of 365 days of the year formed a mean between the numbers 360 and 370. So too for the 36 decans which are intimately tied up with the extra-zodiacal constellations. Their relations with the year of days can be adjusted through the multiplication of 36 and 37, the resultant number 1332 standing as an esoteric symbol of the circle the twelve signs of which each would equate with 111. The half-circle would then be 666.

Now further the typical number of a man is 6, according to tradition. Theologically it is explained as being because he was created on the sixth day. Physically the ideal man is 6 foot in height and with arms outstretched, standing in the ancient attitude of prayer and of the crucifiction, he occupies a square of 6 by 6. Again, a man's ideal limit of age is 72 which exactly equals one degree of the circle of the sun's great year. Man is the Microcosm, Man is the unit.* It may be taken that these numbers with their recurring integers were assumed to the definition of sacred names because of their triadic form. Thrice Great was the epithet applied to Hermes by the Graeco-Egyptians for there were three worlds in the universe, and the trinity was, of course, the figure of power and completion. The number 666 is obviously to be related to the point of the Equinox, that is to say to the place of the Sun's Exaltation, which divides the light and dark halves of the year—the period of the sun's triumph from the winter period of his weakness.

Resuming consideration of the name TEITAN which equiva-

* The Great Year equals 360 men's lives. 360 by 72.

lates with the number 666. The family of Titans were the children of rebellion—they dethroned and emasculated their father Ouranos. Here Hesiod tells one of the strangest of cosmological myths describing the division between heaven and earth and the revolt of Time—Kronos—and his eleven brethren. Hyperion—the sun—was one of those who aided in binding the paternal power, casting the seed of heaven into the ocean. Thence, with the generation of Aphrodite from the sea foam, came into being the lesser forms of life.

After this came the revolt of Zeus. But in astrological notions the two chief figures survived, Time as Saturn, Lord of Night, and Hyperion as Helios the God of Day; equals were they in their power and strength. One had his exaltation in Libra and the other in Aries, opposite signs in the Zodiac, the one the beginning of Autumn, the other the beginning of Spring. They had been resumed to that scheme of stars and planets which came from the Eastern land where, long earlier, their myth had its beginnings. And their successor Zeus—Jupiter—holds his thunders in the sign of Cancer midway between them—the sign of his Mystery—the dawn point in the Thema Mundi of the astrologers—the day of Creation.

Emasculated, infecund Ouranos sleeps in the great circle bounding the world, amidst the fixed stars, like the first man Adam Kadmon—the Macrocosm. As in so many of the myths, there is here, too, a fall from heaven, a fall by way of the lordship of Kronos—the Saturnian divinity—and then to the rule of Zeus, an Olympian, a mere god of mountain and thunder and lightning. Like the Fall in Genesis it began with the defection of the woman. From the Golden Age life fell to the trouble of latter days.

But after Time's conquest of Space comes a new strife. A spirit revives in the world which would escape his tyranny and his sons'. Upon man comes a mystical passion and he seeks freedom. His spirit strives to attain to the primal condition; the vision of a life beyond the bound of shifting stars comes upon the seer; his spirit quickens. He dreams of a great rider with a blood-stained garment and a secret name upon his thigh, who comes riding at the head of the hosts of heaven to the sacred marriage. New-built, reintegrate, tower-crowned, the Holy City standing upon the great circle of the star signs awaits him—his bride, the exalted Venus, the Uranian divinity. Their marriage, which is the wedding of soul and spirit, is also that universal hierogamy, the ancient, prehuman embrace of the Heaven and the Earth.

As our Cabalists have read its number, it is simply, 'Ο ΟΥΡΑΝΟΣ=961='Η ΚΑΙΝΗ 'ΙΕΡΟΥΣΑΛΗΜ

THE HOUSES OF HEAVEN

THE story that is recounted in the Apocalypse has at first sight little sequence in narrative. Yet, on the other hand, the system on which the author worked is quite definite, as the curious series of sevens overrunning both words and symbols evidences. By collation of his symbolical images it is made more and more certain that the whole measure of his myth appertained to things celestial—to the vast revolutions of the stars and the way of soul and spirit therein. Moreover, an instance of substantial correspondence is to be found in the series of astrological symbols called the houses of the heavens when compared with the controlling scheme, or plot, of the Apocalypse.

Regarding St. John's Revelation as of the same type as all other apocalypses, that is, an ascent into the skies, its narrative from the star and candle-lighted vision of the Churches to the ultimate triumph followed by the descent from heaven of the new church as Bride may be compared with the houses of the heavens ascending from beneath the earth to the midheaven. This progression according to the ancient names of the houses goes from the Hypogeion (called also the *Immum Coeli,* the Deep, the place beneath the earth or, in Western astrologers' parlance, the Grave), in other words, the fourth house, to the house called that of Triumph, of Success, and of Honours, the Midheaven and the seventh from this. Beyond is the Ogdoad, the eighth in this order which is the house of Religion.

The order of these houses ascending from the Grave to the house of Honours, using their old names, is as follows:

1. Hypogeion, Below the Earth, *i.e.* the 4th house, Domus Patrimonii.
2. Dea, the Goddess,   the 3rd house, Domus Fortunae.
3. Anaphora, Rising, Coming up, the 2nd house, Domus Lucri.
4. Horoscopos, Visible Boundary, the 1st house, Domus Vitae.
5. Kakodaimon, Evil daemon,   the 12th house, Domus Carceris.
6. Agathodaimon, Good daemon, the   11th   house,   Domus
                               Amicorum.
7. Mesouranema, Midheaven,   the   10th   house,   Domus
                               Honorium and Cor Coeli.
8. Deos, God,   the 9th house, Domus Religionis.

Set out in parallel with the sequence of events in St. John's Revelation it will be remarked that the whole progression hinges on the birth in its characteristic house, the House of Life. It explains the antecedent and consequent events. It is a movement which is distinct from that of the sun in the Zodiac, that is to say the Year movement, but belongs to the day of twenty-four hours, which is in reverse.

The list of signs compared with houses and the seven stages of the Apocalypse is as follows:

The House of the Grave or   The candlesticks; John falls as one dead
        Hypogeion.   and sees the vision of Time, the
                            whitehaired one.

        of Writings or   Seals of the Book of life opened.
        Dea.

        of Wealth or   Trumpets giving announcement of
        Anaphora.   the resurrection.

        of Life or Horo- Thunders giving voice to the New
        scopos.   Birth—Dawn.
        of Bondage or Reapers, the war with the Dragon.
        Kakodaimon.

        of the King's   Vials, the destruction of the Threefold
        Ministers or   city of Babylon.
        Agathodai-
        mon.

of Triumph or   Great Rider triumphing, the throne
Mesouranema.   judgment.
or Cor Coeli.

of Religion or   New Jerusalem, the Church of God.
Deos.

The history begins with the vision of the seven candles in the house
of the Grave, the underworld of darkness. After falling down in a
symbolical death St. John is commanded to write. In the next vision
the seven Seals of the Book of Life are opened. This is in the house of
Writings. Here he sees the loosing of creatures significant of the
underworld who ascend from the abyss.

The third series announces the New Dawn and the end of time
with the blowing of Trumpets. This is the house of uprising, the
Anaphora. Next come the Thunders of the New Birth, the seven
voices of the heavens telling of the spiritual parturition; the man child
is brought forth in the house of Life, the Horoscopos, or in the visible
Hour of the New Dawn.

The fifth series, that of the Reapers, follows on the description of
the flight of the woman to the desert and the war with the dragon.
This is the house of Bondage, Domum Carceris, Kakodaimon.
The sixth series recounts the pouring of the Vials and tells of the fall
of the great city of Babylon. This is the house called Domus
Amicorum, of King's Ministers, and named Agathodaimon.

Seventh is the Last Judgment, the scene of the triumphant
Rider's coming in glory. That appears in the house of Success,
Triumph and Honours, the Cor Coeli which is to say Midheaven—
Mesouranema. This is the house of the Lamb of the Revelation who
has this sevenfold title of honour—"And I beheld, and I heard the
voice of many angels round about the throne and the beasts and the
elders: and the number of them was ten thousand times ten thousand,
and thousands of thousands; saying with a loud voice, Worthy is the
Lamb that was slain to receive power, and riches, and wisdom, and
strength, and honour, and glory, and blessing."

It is a matter of curious interest to compare these seven characteristics of the Lamb, which proceed in an ascending scale, with the
houses. Beginning with blessing in the house of Religion, there is
glory in the house of Triumph, honour in the house of the King's

Ministers, strength in the house of Bondage, wisdom in the house of Life, riches in the house of Wealth, and power in the house of Writings. The preceding characteristic, stating that he was slain, corresponds with the Grave and indicates the purport of the suc‑ ceeding order.

Finally the Eighth, the New Jerusalem, appears in the house of Religion, or Deos, in the astrological house of God. Already at this point the house of midheaven is passed and this house is on the descending arc from the zenith: "John saw the holy city, new Jerusalem coming down from God (deos) out of heaven." (Rev. xxi, 2).

This is not a matter of chance.

PLOTINUS AND HERMES

"*INCREASE thyself to immeasurable height, leaping clear of all body and surmounting all time, become eternal and thou shalt know God. There is nothing impossible to thyself. Deem thyself immortal and able to do all things . . . . become higher than all Height, and lower than all Depth . . . . to be everything at the same time in earth and sea and heaven. Think that thou art as yet begotten, that thou art in the womb, that thou art young, that thou art old, that thou hast died and art beyond death: perceive all these things together . . . . and thou shalt know God. But if thou shuttest up thy soul in thy body, and abasest thyself and sayest 'I know nothing, I can do nothing, I am afraid of earth and sea, I cannot mount to heaven, I know not what I was or what I shall be; then what hast thou to do with God?*" (Corpus Hermeticum xi. (ii).)*

PLOTINUS offers a method of interior vision for the purpose of obtaining that ecstatic union which means harmony with the system of the universal spirit in life. The quotation is taken from his essay "On Intelligible Beauty":—

"Let us, then, form a mental image of this cosmos with each of its parts remaining what it is, and yet interpenetrating one another (imagining) them all together into one as much as we possibly can—so that whatsoever one comes first into the mind as the 'one' (as for instance the outer sphere), there immediately follows also the sight of the semblance of the sun, and together with it that of the outer stars, and the earth, and sea, and all things living, as though in (one) transparent sphere—in fine, as though all things could be seen in it.

"Let there, then, be in the soul some semblance of a sphere of light (transparent) having all things in it, whether moving or still, or some of them moving and others still.

"And holding this (sphere) in the mind, conceive in thyself another (sphere), removing (from it all idea of) mass; take from it also (the idea of) space, and the phantom of matter in thy mind; and do not try to image another sphere (merely) less in bulk than the former.

"Then invoking God who hath made (that true sphere) of which thou holdest the phantom (in thy mind), pray that He may come.

" And may He come with his own cosmos, with all the Gods therein—He being one and all, and each one all, united into one, yet different in their powers, and yet, in that one (power) of multitude all one.

"Nay, rather the One God is all (the Gods) for that He falleth not short (of Himself) though all of them are (from Him); (and) they are all together yet each again apart in (some kind of) an unextended state, possessing no form perceptible to sense.

" For, otherwise, one would be in one place, another in another, and (each be) 'each,' and not 'all' in itself, without parts other from the others and (other) from itself.

" Nor is each whole a power divided and proportioned according to a measurement of parts; but this (whole) is the all, all power, extending infinitely and infinitely powerful;—nay, so vast is that (divine world-order), that even its 'parts' are infinite."*

The language and terms are at first sight difficult but in short it may be understood that the way to the divine vision is to be gained by a full understanding of the interrelated spheres of the heavens and a true inward comprehension of them. The process implies an enhancement of the power of visualizing to an intense degree and the effective-

* G. R. S. Mead's translation.

ness of its operation would depend pre-eminently on the pure faculty of mental imagery—a clear imagination. The cosmos that great harmony must be imaged and patterned within the seeker for union with its Great Soul.

And moreover a description of this method of arriving at the state necessary for true contemplation of the Divine is given according to Hermes Trismegistus. He discourses to Tat upon the "Six-and-thirty Decans" and their activity:

"This should prove the most authoritative sermon and the chiefest of them all." He continues: "We have already spoken unto thee about the Circle of the Animals, or the Life-giving One, of the Five Planets, and of the Sun and Moon, and of the circle (or sphere) of each one of these" and again "we said, son, there is a Body which encompasses all things. Conceive it then, as being in itself a kind of figure of spherelike shape: so is the universe conformed." Tat responds "I've thought of such a figure in my mind, just as thou dost describe, O Father mine."*

Then after a long discourse upon the functions of these heavenly powers and their relation to man Hermes says:

" Such is the nature of the stars. The Stars, however, differ from the star groups. The stars are they which sail in heaven; the star groups, on the contrary, are fixed in heaven's frame, and they are borne along together with the heavens—Twelve out of which we call the Zodia. He who knows these can form some notion clearly of what God is: and, if one should dare to say so, becoming thus a seer for himself, so contemplate Him, and, contemplating Him, be blessed."

Tat replies:

"Blessed, in truth, is he of the Father, who contemplateth Him." Then Hermes says: "But 'tis impossible, O Son, that one in body should have this good chance. Moreover, he should train his soul beforehand, here and now, that when it reacheth there (the space) where it is possible for it to contemplate, it may not miss its way. But men who love their bodies—such men will never contemplate the vision of the Beautiful and Good."

Here is manifestly a rite of self-initiation into the great movement

* G. R. S. Mead "Thrice greatest Hermes" for this and succeeding quotations from the Hermetic books.

of the world and one which depends upon some knowledge of the stars and their heavenly spheres. Man gains a vision of the divinity of the universe by means of clarifying its image within him—in other terms that he gets outside the world sphere. So does the good charioteer of Plato, for in Phaedrus is described the journey in the way of the Gods upon the outer sphere of the heavens to be borne round by its revolution and to gaze on the *external scene*.

But Plotinus in his essay on the Ecstasy of the Final Beauty goes on to say:

"To those that do not see entire, the immediate impression is alone taken into account; but those drunken with this wine, filled with the nectar, all their souls penetrated by this beauty, cannot remain mere gazers: no longer is there a spectator outside gazing on an outside spectacle; the clear-eyed hold the vision within themselves, though, for the most part, they have no idea that it is within but look towards it as to something beyond them and see it as an object of vision caught by a direction of the will.

"All that one sees as a spectacle is still external; one must bring the vision within and see no longer in that mode of separation but as we know ourselves; thus a man as filled with a god—possessed by Apollo or by one of the Muses—need no longer look outside for his vision of the divine being; it is but finding the strength to see divinity within."

"*LET us then make a mental picture of our universe: each member shall remain what it is, distinctly apart; yet all is to form, as far as possible, a complete unity so that whatever comes into view shall show as it were the surface of the orb over all, bringing immediately with it the vision, on the one plane, of the sun and of all the stars with earth and sea and all living things as if exhibited upon a transparent globe.*

"*Bring this vision actually before your sight, so that there shall be in your mind the gleaming representations of a sphere, a picture holding all the things of the universe moving or in repose or (as in reality) some at rest, some in motion. Keep this sphere before you, and from it imagine another, a sphere stripped of magnitude and of spatial differences; cast out your inborn sense of Matter, taking care not merely to attenuate it: call on God, maker of the sphere whose image you now hold, and pray Him to enter. And may He come bringing His own Universe with all the Gods that dwell in it.—He who is the one God and all the Gods, where each is all, blending into a unity, distinct in powers but all one God in virtue of that one divine power of many facets." (Trans. Stephen Mackenna).*

THE SEVEN MYTHS

WHEN it is considered that the attitude of a man standing with arms outstretched and body erect is, properly speaking, the ancient ritual position of prayer, some conception of its purport in the revelation of last things may be gained. Clearly when this mystical attitude is taken the head is towards the height of heaven the feet towards the deeps, which is that the head is uplifted to the North and the feet set below in the South. Not bowed down but erect—such is the attitude of worship taken by one who, with some dignity, would look upon the Great Æon and see in him his own spirit. Thus was it done in a noble and antique fashion looking towards the north stars.

With his body set towards the four corners of the world on the day of the Lord so the seer awaited the voice of the Clamator and then as he said, turning about, he fell as one dead. He had faced the great figure, seeing first the seven candles about the feet below and, above them, that terrific figure filling the sky. Looking upwards into the flaming eyes of the *Cosmocrator* he fell back like a stricken man.

And so lying regarding the immense being with the north stars in its hand—the tremendous vision of the whole fiery life of the circling universe—the seer himself would lie extended as if he were its counterpart. His feet, too, would be set beneath Libra, deep among the stars of the centaurs where the sacrifice of the strange beast was offered at the altar below. Flaming feet were they, burning feet of brass to trample the all-bedamned. And up from that depth lies their path beside the grim Hydra whilst in the north was the mighty Dragon about his mentor's breast. So stretched out, with back to the earth, looking into the fulness of heaven, regarding from South to North, then to the seer's right hand would be west, and to his left east.

But for the *summus genius* the reverse would be the case and his right hand—in which are the seven spirits of God, counterparts of the seven planets—is in the midst holding the stars of the north, those of the little Bear, uplifted in blessing.

An ascent through and within himself—In himself as micro-cosmic and the image and pattern of the cosmos, the heavens move stage by stage from his right hand towards his left; the motion in his counterpart's is from the left hand conversely. And with this movement from the seer's left hand, at each change the purifying visions from the seven spirits appear and sweep across like great angels in bands of seven. Yet, at the same time, swinging over the arms of the cross on which he has extended himself until in the end it rests upon each hand, moves the great stream of the Galaxy like' a rain of gold. When the Seals are opened it appears flowing along the north-west towards the right hand in the sign Gemini and in the West; and when the New Jerusalem appears finally, it stretches across the middle of heaven from the sign of the Horseman, Sagittarius, to the sign of the Twins, Gemini, in the East.

If a succession of crosses is set out upon the sky of constellations, the particular myth associated with each appearance of a new order of signs becomes more definite. Taking first the aspect of the heavens when Libra is at the south point; the mighty Æon, who appears as the bearer of the seven promises of the spirits, or gifts of Paradise, has, as background, the precise star figures which explain the strange saying repeated several times in St. John's Gospel that the son of man must be lifted up even "as Moses lifted up the serpent in the wilderness." Now this, of course, refers to the setting of the brazen serpent on a pole to save the people of Israel who were being tormen-ted and destroyed by the stinging reptiles in the desert-wandering.

Such a figure, plainly, is expressed in this aspect of the heavens, for the *stauros* of the cross has at its zenith the great star group of Draco, and all about the horizon on each side of its foot are the figures of reptiles, Serpens, Hydra and Scorpio. Nevertheless it is amid these monsters that the figure of the great and fiery spirit appears—the actuating life of the world bearing the assurance of the sevenfold reward for endurance. This Æon figure is, of course, the vision of Phanes, the primary genesis of light, the cosmic ruler who holds the polestars in his hand. He is guarding the paradisial tree of knowledge and he has the Keys of Death and Hades. In Hades his feet are set and in paradise is his right hand.

Before the second vision unfolds John is caught up to the door of heaven and sees him again—or one like to him seated on a Throne with the seven-sealed book in his hand. And he hears that the Lion, the first of the Living Creatures, has prevailed to open it. But the Lamb, Aries, comes out from the north to perform the opening. So is introduced the coming forth of the figures manifested at the opening of the Seals of the Book of Fate who indicate the traversal of the underworld.

In the great constellation Hydra is set the foot of this Cross of the seven Seals. Hydra, the great serpent figure of the southern depth, stretches, together with the two centaurs, right across the sky from East horizon to West horizon. In this abyss of the underworld where stands the Altar of sacrifice, are the strange horsemen, for this is the mystical Valley of the Centaurs, from which they ride up to the gate of the city above.

When the heavens have been moved and the sun and moon darkened at the opening of the sixth Seal, the four winds are held and the Tribes of Israel are sealed to God. Then is the seventh Seal opened and there comes a great Silence marvellous and strange. . . After that, fire is cast on the earth from the altar before the throne and the Trumpeters are prepared. At the end of the torments that the six Trumps had produced, the four angels bound in Euphrates, the great river, are released. Thereafter, whilst the great smoke of a burning world arises, the great angel appears who is accompanied by the seven secret Thunders and who is clothed with clouds.

Here begins the myth of the Seventh and Last Trump, the call to resurrection. It tells of the eating of a little book by John, like Ezekiel had done before him, and also of the measuring of the holy place and the holy of holies, and of the altar. There is an account of the two prophets who were two candles, and two olive trees, in the city called Sodom, and of Egypt where their Lord was crucified.

Now the seven Trumps sound when the foot of the cross in the circle of heaven stands beneath Leo and, therefore, also, the horses of woe from the abyss have faces of lions and the angel garbed in clouds has a lion's voice. And after this sound the seven Thunders.

They, and the Last Trump, announce the opening of the

Tabernacle of God in heaven. This is the rending of the veil announced by the Thunders and trumpets at the crucifiction, for this is the mystical revelation of the secret hidden by the cloud and the lightning flash. That which germinated in the womb of earth, of Semele—in the bosom of the goddess of Hades, Persephone—the cherished seed, now comes to birth in a sign of mighty wonder in heaven. Here is recounted the great myth of the Woman and the Dragon, declaring the secret of the cross of seven Thunders, the mystery for which Time has been waiting and for which the world has been in travail. Now is the last barrier passed. The hidden things of the ark of the testimony are made plain in this history of the war of Michael with the dragon who, as Hydra, is driven back from the foot of the cross. For this cross of the secret Thunders stands in the sign Cancer and its stem is in the great ship Argo, the ark, whilst its arms extend from the Balance (Michael's symbol) to the sign rising in the west, Aries.

After this the angel messengers are heard flying through heaven and the great cosmic reaping takes place, the harvesting of the corn, and the vine of the Earth is trodden without the city. The city of heaven is surrounded by the twelve gates, or the castles, the houses of the Zodiac. And the stem of this cross of the Reapers stands in Gemini, which is the Gateway with the twin pillars. Here is the place of the dragon's head in Astrology and here, in the Apocalyptic myth of the Great Winepress, the blood ran deep as the horses' bridles for sixteen hundred *stadia*.

Appearing from the temple, garbed in *stone,* seven angels who bear the Vials are appointed to the drama of the Fall of Babylon. Into the wilderness the saint was carried in the spirit to see the great harlot seated on the scarlet Beast, for this is the mystery which is accomplished in the Last Judgment. And the seven Vial bearers pour out that which was begun by the Trumpeters, whose destructions were of exactly the same kind. For the sixth poured out on the Euphrates in each and the last on the air and then a voice cried out from the throne of heaven itself saying "It is done." This Cross of the Seven Vials stands in Taurus, with Leo and Aquarius —the water-pourer—on its arms.

And at the Last Judgment is recounted of the great war in heaven, as the Great Rider leads the white-robed Hosts of Heaven in

F

conquest—the hosts here equate with those from the abyss when the cross stood in the Lion—and the Cross of the Angels of Judgment stands in Aries, the sign of the Lamb.

This then, is the sequence of the myths of the seven crosses under these titles or descriptions:—

First is the Vision of the Great Æon standing amongst the candle-sticks and surrounded by serpents.

Second are the Centaurs, the great Riders, and the Altar in the Underworld.

Third—The Silence, the Angel with the little book, the Two witnesses and the Seventh Trump.

Fourth—The Woman, the Child, Michael and the three dragons.

Fifth—The Reaping of the harvest and the treading of the Wine-press.

Sixth—The Great City of Whoredoms, Babylon, and her Cup of Fornications.

Seventh—The Rider on the white horse in blood-stained raiment and the conquering hosts in white.

Last—The New Jerusalem, The Bride, and the Golden Queen-City of the New Age.

THE ORB OF THE WORLD

AT the last St. John the Divine is carried away in the Spirit to the summit of the mystical mountain and there he sees a wonderful and marvellous vision. A city founded upon the symbols of the Twelve Zodiacal constellations descends to be the Bride of the conquering Rider on the white horse. But is there this only as an end, that a tower-crowned woman—a purified and beatified City-Goddess—should espouse a man divine, a priest-king clad in blood-stained raiment? Have the vast cosmic movements, the world disasters and ruining burning rains from heaven culminated in so simple a matter? Hardly indeed, did Babylon fall for this only, Babel, the Queen City, the world's wonder. Something, it would seem, more universal is necessarily implied in this marked and obvious grouping of symbols.

When John, Master of Secret Wisdom, Astrologer, Alchemist, ascended in the spirit for this last and fourth time, he was lifted up by an Angel, one of those seven who poured the Vials—perhaps the last of them, whose sign is the mystical urn-bearer, Aquarius, and whose Royal Star is in the Fish's mouth. From that high place, the mountain of the Lord, he saw the whole array of the Twelve signs of the Zodiac dominating the horizon. He was set in the midst, standing as if on the dragon who is the centre of the Ecliptic, and saw it in full circle about him in every quarter.

Of course, such as he saw it, it was a new world, for no more were the circles askew. The path of the erring stars, as it should, now moves true to the rest, and Earth and Heaven move at one, progressing in a perfect fullness of order. Change of season can no more exist, nor the dragon car of Demeter drive through the heavens bringing times of plenty and dearth. And in the new city the great Tree in the midst bears twelve fruits for the parts of the year.

From this may be discerned a broader purport through consideration of the constellation figures indicated. Extending from to East and to West is the Galaxy, flowing from midheaven as the river of the water of life. And at the signs to which it streams down East and West are the points of intersection for Galaxy with Zodiac. Moreover these are the significant places where are the exaltations of the Dragon's Head and Tail, that is, the *nodes,* crucial points of intersection in the paths of sun and moon. Here are the signs of Gemini and Sagittarius—of the Twins and of the Man-horse—the Centaur— who tramples the crown of the underworld. Here is the critical point, the hinge, the pivot where all may be done or undone.

Such is the Master Vision of the secret of the spirit's triumph. Now is the Zodiacal circle set true to the horizon and the foundations of the holy city are fixed level. For how otherwise may it come down and rest secure upon the twelve signs. As they are pitched and move normally, it would stand awry, wallowing like a storm-shaken ship. And to do this the great golden Draco must be set on the turning point not only as he is, as centre of the Ecliptic, but upon the very pivot of the stars—transfixed on the pole itself. For his are the errant seven. He (and the planets also) had left their appointed place, setting the heavens askew, throwing down a third part of the stars, a truly Chaldean notion. The Dragon had wandered away, he was rocking the universe.

Through their aberration came that swing—"the nodding of the pole" out of true, that changes it point by point amongst the middle stars in a circle of 26,000 little years—which is the great year of the Polar motion and the sun's return. All this is caused, as we know, by the drag upon the earth of the sun and moon, its fellows in this dance of worlds.

At the moment then that the Heavenly River of Stars, the Galaxy, rests on the horizon East and West, were but the head and tail of the dragon Draco set again in the great stream, the Divine equinox would be on that instant; for then the pole would be back in its true place in the summit of the Galaxy's arch of Fire. That Burning Fence, the boundary of the universe, was never counted of old amongst the constellations; it was esteemed a great principle and a mysterious force in being. As the Holy stream of Life and the Divine Road it was bond and bound of the great world, the golden cord that tied the universe together into one whole. A myth, of course.

All the old myths tell how that the world had been shaken on a time and that things afterwards went all askew. Something had happened in heaven, a revolt of angels, or a son who had dethroned the father. Separation and division had come about and with that was strife and wrong between men. For the Age of Gold was over and a varying of seasons came with that, and so excess of cold and heat and garments and shame, and disturbing desire, and passion and sick longings, labour and weariness. And now in the triumph of the spirit the pivot was set upright—the twist taken out of things, the pole erect, vertical.

In the very Zenith, at this instant of success, overthrown, cast head-long down is Cassiopeia, the wicked queen—hurled down like Jezebel. For the blood-splashed horseman is come, driving furiously like Jehu, and there in the burning crown of the arch is the constella-tion where she sat—the Throne. So in his ancient place again at the summit of the great orb of the world encoiled about the throne and the pole is the dragon once again. Now spins all truly, for the great circle of living creatures move as guardians along the edge of the world's horizon.

Here then is the grand myth about which the most eminent of Divines, John, set all the learning of his age. It tells of the storming of heaven by the great horseman, the ascent of the spirit of man triumphing over the cosmic tyrants who delight in wanton change. Therewith, too, is the casting down of the wicked Queen and the winning of a bride.

In Man the book of life is, just as it is in the great world, an order of conditions—of states of being—and upon this Book, upon the life in man, are set the seals of the seven griping masters. We know that in man the blood is the life and that the life in the blood is spirit. What then is this conflict amidst the stars and by which the life— the Spirit—the "I" finds itself?

Bound in the circle of life (that is, in the Zodiac, which, of course, has its parallel in system with the body and life of man) the spirit continues in the rule of that world which the seven have arranged for it. And except by the Spirit's discovery of the purport of the strange bonds upon the circle wherein it is imprisoned fatally, it continues to move through the appointed forms of living therein. But the circle of stars, the book of life itself, bears in the character imaged on it the resolution of the problem. In this living movement there is separation and difference from the vaster motion of the upper heaven: the part has its distinction from the whole. It sags and reels somewhat about the little native world of earth. Swayed by the diverse powers of the lesser stars its masters, it is changeful and suffers from excess of laws and rulers, dominated by the seven planets whose central star symbol is the golden dragon, Draco. The circle of its life marked amongst the stars as the Zodiac was seen by the ancient cosmologists as erring— they looked in it for the psychological image of defect—for they felt that its path meant a falling off from and abandonment of true and faithful order.

At two points then this wheel of becoming—rocking ever above and below the plane of the horizon—is crossed by the Galactic stream, and there are set the points of the *exaltation* and *fall* of the Dragon's head and tail. These are marked by the great biformed symbols Gemini and Sagittarius. Here it would seem are the gates which lead out of the whirl of becoming.

John in the spirit was shown first the vision of the seven candles and next that of the throne and the seven-sealed book, symbolical images of the seven planets. He saw the four great Beasts about the throne, the emblems of the signs of the four Royal Stars. They called out "Come and see" at the awful opening of the deeps of being. Sagittarius appeared the first symbol of the descent into the under-world: other horsemen followed, Hades pursuing after the fourth who was Death. Hades was that altar beneath which tarried those souls who, crying out, were given white garments and told to wait awhile. It stands deep in the southern heavens and from it flows ever upward the stream of the Galaxy like the smoke of the burning from a fire of sacrifice. Here is consummated the rite which the centaurs perform among the lowest stars. And then sun and moon are darkened and in the Silence of Heaven the gate is passed. The seventh seal has been opened, its sign has been reached; Gemini is the door to the upward way of the gods.

Thus then, descending into the underworld like a hero riding, the spirit sets forth on the passage through Hades, conquering and to conquer. He joins in the strange sacrifice in the deep and thereafter in the end leads the hosts of souls to victory in his blood-spattered garment. And the two double signs, Twins and Man-horse, indicate the two gates into and out of the world below. So again Gemini suggests the two paths to choose, the one mounting to heaven the Galaxy, the other to continue in the circle of the Zoa, the Zodiac wherein the spirit of man lies bound like a great king in prison.

Soul and spirit have their places in these two circles of life, and therefore it is at this point the seer sees his Genius—or the Son of Man —amid clouds and the voices of seven thunders cry their secret messages to him. Here begins the new world and the strife with the dragon. For the ark of promise is opened, the mystical child is born —the Branch who comes is it perhaps, from that budded almond rod which was hidden there? And the brazen serpent, was that there too? This is the moment of resurrection, the seventh Trumpet has blown for the raising of the dead. The almond is the ancient symbol of regeneration both for Gentile and Jew.

Later comes the Judgment, and Babel is condemned and the bridal vision is seen, for Spirit and Soul are united as the balance of the world is renewed. The ascent is complete and the seer's spirit stands on the holy mountain great and high. The golden waters pour now from the midst of the heavens' circle. True and unwavering stands the wall of signs about its edge whilst the dragon is drenched in the fiery waters of life—impaled on the pole—glorified in the very midst.

Such a significant completion indicates the sources of the myth about which all moves. With the seven stars in his hand and the seven stars about his feet the first figure sufficiently indicates the final motive. White-haired with burning feet and shining face like the sun, he is the primary typical master of Time, Pater Bromios, or the Orphic Eros—Phanes the light-bringer—He is the bearer of the keys. With a lion's flaming face he holds the pole like a staff in his one hand; with the stars or the thunders in the other, and a serpent twined about him, he is the Zervan Akarana—Time unending—of the Persian East. The Æon is accompanied by the four primal winds of the royal stars, for he is the Lord of the Spirit of Life flashing from south to north as the central original light and fire of the great world. His naturally is to guard the throne on the summit of the north from which Daniel saw the fiery river stream down. Ezekiel saw him too, and all the mystics, even to Pascal who drew a flaming cross at the head of his note his "memorial" where he wrote down with the heading "Fire" the date and hour of his revelation and sewed it in his garment.

All the secret is told in the three mysteries of the father, Kronos, of the son, Zeus and the Queen Aphrodite: Saturn of the Judgment, Jupiter of the Thunders, and Venus of the Mirror of Life. So is the mystery of Babylon the key to that of the seven planets. They are the rulers of the life of Man, lesser Gods and masters of his Fate. It is the mystery of Jezebel—Babel—who said "I sit a Queen, and am no Widow, and shall see no sorrow"—of Venus who is Libitina and Urania both.

"And here *is* the mind which hath wisdom," as St. John the Divine wrote, seeming to smile towards his fellow stargazers dreaming with him in the sacred night long sober drunkenness of the watchers of the heavens. "The seven heads are seven mountains, on which the woman sitteth. And there are seven kings: five are fallen, and one is, and the other is not yet come;—and the beast that was and is not, even he is the eighth."

For the kings were those who had sealed the book of fate, setting their bonds upon the spirit. And when the last of these was broken and the evil city destroyed, then could the Saint—the Holy One in man, the "I" indivisible—ascend to the mountain of the Lord, the throne on the summit where already sat the Father and the Son.

This indeed was the place to be won by the apotheosis of man's spirit, for it is the winning of a part in divinity that is promised by the Alpha and Omega. The third place on the Throne is for him that overcometh; nothing less is the reward as John expounds it in the seven promises made to the seven churches—the ecclesia—the seven centres of faith. He defines the seven gifts which are characteristic of the reintegrated Paradise in this New Eden, telling of the exemplary rewards granted to the spiritually true, of the seven virtues of the starry spirits of God burning before the Throne. Beginning with the Tree of Life of Alpha, they go on through the order of seven sacred vowels. Perhaps they are the secret contents of the Ark of the Testimony, for amongst them is offered the hidden Manna which Paul said was put there; was also the rod that budded the stem from which came the Tree of Life? Or, in the ark, was the testimony—the witness—that of which the secret Thunders told, and therefore were sealed up, and was the little book of double taste the law written on the stones therein?

Beginning then, first, with Alpha: the Spirit holding the seven stars declared to Ephesus that he that overcometh shall eat of the Tree of Life: to Smyrna "The first and the last, who was dead and lives again" declared that he shall not be hurt of the Second Death: to Pergamum "he that hath the two edged sword" offers the hidden manna and a white stone and a new and secret name. To Thyatira "The Son of God with flaming eyes and feet like burnished brass "promises the Morning Star and a rod of iron to rule nations: to Sardis from "Him that hath the seven spirits of God" are offered white garments and a name unblotted in the Book of Life: to Philadelphia by Him that hath the key of David" is promised to be a pillar in the Temple of God and have written on him three divine names: and last to Laodicea "the Amen the true witness the beginning of Creation," gives as reward to sit down on the throne with the Son and the Father.

With the first seal when the power of the Moon, Alpha, "that works increase and decrease" is broken, comes the gift of eating the fruit of the Tree of Life that is renewed every month in the year. When the second bond, that of the Sun, is broken and "arrogance, fire-faced" is overcome, the spirit is not to be hurt of the Second Death which (according to Plutarch) means renewed life in some form of material body. With an end of the power of Mercury," evil cunning," the spirit is given the Hidden Manna and the White Stone. As "lust whereby men are deceived," the power of Venus is broken; he gains the Morning Star and the Ruling Sceptre. From overcoming "the force of unholy and rash audacity" in Mars he gains to remain in the Book of Life, and leaving with Jupiter "striving for wealth and power," he becomes a Pillar with three divine names written on it. Finally, with freedom from Saturn's character of "falsehood that lies in wait to work harm," he is given the seat of Spiritual Wisdom, the third place on the Divine Throne.

SPIRIT AND SOUL

AFTER all, it is primarily as a work of art that the Apocalypse endures. To call it great prophecy is, in fact, to say that it is great poetry. This really is the element of truth—truth as we know it—which survives; it is the sole thing having an eternal verity. It has in it the element of permanence. And despite the obscurity in which the Apocalyptic scheme and its dramatic order always, apparently, has been enveloped, it has maintained its place in the Canon.

And whoever reads it with proper aesthetic sensibility has always found therein that authentic thrill which moves to the true ecstasy. So powerful has been its effect that many sincere and religious readers have felt that the afflatus communicated by the great poet, its author, was an immediate revelation of the divine purposes—which they commonly translated into premonitions of forthcoming disasters. Reading it they confounded its poetic wonders with the simple astronomical numbers and figures used to define its mechanism, symbols themselves in a minor order and employed to coordinate and regularise the vaster powers of myth and vision to the strict order of his drama.

Such a remarkable work is it indeed, that despite all difficulties, all obscurities, all riddles, its symbols are established deep in our habit of thought. Revealing in the marvels of a vision in the moving heavens the essential order and form which belongs to our ritual and to its congeners, it possesses at once so human and yet so universal a character that its images have been found most oddly adapted to the recondite and preposterous fancies of hairbrained students as well as the most dignified and profound expressions of the learned.

But whatever there may be of the prodigious in its presentation, it possesses the greater quality of a fundamental simplicity in primary motive which has served to keep it from decay. Through a supremely splendid order of myth and astronomical figure develops this unique motive. It expounds that which inheres in every one of us—that which is and which makes all art and all drama, the very stuff of life which populates the world within as the world without.

The Apocalypse reveals then the two interior powers in man— the two selves. It recounts their strife, their divagations, their passions and their marriage. This is the traditional Hierogamia—the holy, the mystical, the celestial. Its subject is the war between the one, that is, the ego—and the many, that multiplex which is called in the world within, the psyche. Conflict is waged between object and subject, between simplicity and diversity, and all is there expressed with the comprehensive finality of the noblest art.

Within each and all of us is the never-ending reaction of forces, the secrets of which John reveals in terms of the cosmic movement. It is Nature that pours forth the swarming host of changeful images, and the awakened spirit in man must strive with the outrush to command, lest, in the turmoil, that balance of reason should fail which is his force and power.

Creative, darkling, the spirit would rule, consolidate, order, clarify, even to diminishing, all that the progenitive soul desires merely to increase as swarming images and vague repetitions. Accumulating thoughts and images about it as properties, the soul is the mother of memory, gathering and losing, heaping up and hiding away in secret places. It shelters itself amongst these objects of its desire. But once awakened reborn into new life from the womb of the psyche the regenerated spirit declines to remain in this place of refuge. He is the new man, the regenerate Adam, bursting out from the mean commerce of pawnbroking realities, of bargaining for things outworn.

To the ancient way of thought the spirit is the maker building, shaping; it gives form and consistence, setting up values. That the soul may be saved from the multitude of its productions and their corruption, the spirit must rise up and conquer it and them. He must dominate it as a child dominates its mother, master it as a lover his mistress, rule it as a father his household. And the soul strives to cherish this storming spirit like a child in her bosom, like a sick man in her bed, to devote herself to it as to a father in the grave. She would worship and overwhelm. Upon these two in conflict and in reconciliation is established the subject of the eternal matter of art. Without the two there is nothing, for spirit has no enduring power in time except in its relation with soul.

And the "Fall" of man is the original absorption and conquest of the spirit by the soul—the spirit lulled to sleep in her bosom. From the side of the sleeping Adam went forth Eve. But that true Adam, the bisexed protoplasmic man, sleeps yet. He is still dormant in this world of dual things, obeying the impulses of Eve who is but the half. All the multitudinous shapes, the swarming monsters, grotesques and chimeras of life, all its forms of illusion are but the teeming genera-tions of Psyche—the Soul of the world. Only by the waking of the true Daemon in every man can they be resolved into order.

But once quickened in her, the spirit takes and disciplines with a rod of iron that multitude of her procreations; the half-sexed, half-formed things that she has brought forth. Just as in the womb the germ-plasm of the father, the life-seed, gives shape to the otherwise formless flux, even in the same way does spirit set laws and give order to the universe. So then, in the interior life of each and every human is the stage set for the drama where "I" is the subject and the "ME" the object. For the "I" is the One and the "ME" is the Many. Here we are in that hidden secret world where the subject must be Lord.

All those traits which the line of mothers transmit to their off-spring—all that which links with the body and the making of the body, and which belongs to the period in the womb while the child lives and grows by the mother's blood stream—that is the dominion of the soul. And it is the world of the ancestors and the shades. Yet, from the spirit and by and through the spirit came the urge that abides in the body's mid-point—in the umbilicus—controlling the separation, maintaining the distinction. For this is the original place of conception and fecundation, the seed point, the midmost about which gestation occurs. Here is the way—the channel of communication—from mother to child. And the controlling seed of the father occupies the path between the mother and the growing foetus in her womb.

Dominant, the male plasm is instigator and controller, giving the spirit that lives in the blood. Providing the first impulse to individual life, from it comes also the enduring impulsion to living. Even at the end in the breakdown of the body it has the air of withdrawing to its own place. And in one of its aspects it is Conscience, as, also, it is consciousness.

Things of the spirit then are those of the "I," of the individual which bounds with the Dionysiac pulse of the blood in the dance with the soul. But alone it is Apollo, the One. To the soul is the lymphatic vehicle and all that is possessive in the personal and the ME. The soul is negative and receptive, indecisive, vague, but the spirit is positive and decisive though, lacking soul, its communion with the outer world is inhibited, for the spirit is individual and as such, irresponsive.

Man is not saved by the soul. Indeed it is the soul which needs and clamours for salvation. Moreover often enough, having absorbed and wholly destroyed its own spirit, it will wander like a famished vampire the round of cults and churches vainly crying out for the gift of spirit and wailing in an immitigable blasphemy the name of Jesus. But it is through the interior pure will, by the spirit birth within the soul, that salvation comes. Not by a spirit from outside—from without enter in the diabolical seven—but from within comes the awakening, the cry in the night. Through the strife of spirit and through the pangs of the soul's parturition comes full assurance of life. Spirit is awakened in a flash, but the soul conquers and is conquered only by long labours. The soul is to be saved and the spirit is its saviour unless, as it may be, the *persona*, the soul, has mothered the spirit to its extinction. For the soul can be—and is—the terrible mother destroying through fear.

Through all forms of living creatures run these two, each warring on the other, striving each for mastery—the soul by soft shapes of desire and deceit, the spirit by hard driving order and rule and blind logic. It is in sleep that we best know the soul, for the dream is the way of the soul, living in memory, and we are aware of it as the vague superimposition of images half ordered in awaking by the spirit.

Such is the tradition from old; Man adds his urge to the woman's blood, sealing its stream as his own in the *omphalos* of the new creature. In her join all the ancestral shades to the making of the embryo building the body, informing the soul. And the great drama of Revelation needs must deal with all things even to the sacred mystery of the seed, that which is foe to and conqueror of the dragon. Yet interwoven with it ever and always is the great transmutation which is called death and resurrection. Within—in ourselves—are all these things to be revealed, as in that cup of the mysteries, its dark wine spangled with celestial fire, which is the draught of the king. And in the sacred mirror of love, in his soul, man may discern the greater world and know its secret, finding there the unknown who is nearer than all things else, too close to see, too near to know. Many are its names, it is the divine and universal genius of life, the anti-self, the Daemon, foe and friend, both or either. This is the life that persists even beyond (or in) the divine fireflood, that God cannot and will not destroy, for it is himself.

So whenever man is moved to that great and splendid and triumphal progress through the swarm of images that Time and Memory fling about him both outwardly and inwardly,—whenever by setting the seal of his judgment upon them he turns their disarray into the rank and rule of his spirit, then comes into being the matter of great drama.

Strange names have been given to this great movement in man's mind and its strife with the visible world. Not simply or only has it been expressed in poetry or drama though always has it been taken as the great and whole and true thing of Art. Yet according to the way of thought of the percipient, according to his means and method, it has received various designations. In the Apocalypse it is the Last Judgment and is set around the unsealing of the books of Fate. But the name of it is life and death, though the old Egyptians told of it in the Book of the Dead—of the dead awakened—The Book of Coming Forth by Day. And to Dante it was the Inferno, Purgatorio and Paradiso of the Divine Comedy. It may be called too the tale of Eros and Psyche as in Apuleius, or again, the Banquet of the Gods.

It is the Magnum Opus, the Great Work of the Alchemist—

seen in his Alembic, the Philosophers' Egg; so, too, is it the Divine
Equinox for the Magician—the vision in the House of Gold—for
it is every great travail of the human mind. That which goes on in the
mind of man is that which has gone on eternally in Creation—the
Word spoken and the Light breaking forth, the spirit brooding on the
changeful waters of the great sea of the psyche.

But too long has that increasing vagueness in theologers and
lexicographers confounded spirit and soul together into an inform,
inchoate mass, in this as in so much else, wandering more and ever
more into confusion. Yet though they give us nothing firm and clear
to establish our understanding of this matter, the ordinary usages of
speech tell sufficiently well of the distinction between the two. We
know that which is spirited has, in our everyday talk, a very definite
distinction from the soulful.

For the soul is the habitation of memories recipient of forms, it is
the treasury of the ancestors, the sea wherein are the dead—the
innumerable, the multitudinous dead. And the spirit: why, that is of
air and of fire, a light flashing forth and a great voice crying out! It is
the primal and originating thing, the first as it is the last. Spirit is
vivid, swift and enduring, its life is transmundane, eternal and out of
time. But enwrapped in the womb of the psyche, drawn down from
the starry overworld, it is moribund. So it sleeps in the entangling
web of the garment of dreams woven by the psyche, who is in love
with time and generates therefrom that multiplicity of images called
life. And only by a passion equal to or even like death may we issue
from its many-pictured chambers. Only through the vision of the
seer can we find that divine passion for simplicity. All this is to be
attained by seeking out the veritable creative seed which we have as
the paternal inheritance within and beyond all—beyond the mothers
and across the dream.

Just, then, as the spirit is air and fire, so is the soul earth and sea.
In them are found the four ancient and holy elements, and such is their
division—symbols of their vehicle and rule. Generation is of the soul—
of earth and water—delighting in swarming births. But the spirit
belongs to the stars and is of the makers of time, for its life is in space.
And the soul, like all things living in Time, is changeful, fearing
death, for the soul in its fall brought death into being.

When the spirit, though long lulled to sleep in the soul's bosom comes at the end to awake, then is there death in the soul; mystical, or real, the pang of dissolution is there. Eros or Death is there—the twins. Thus comes the sting of that dying into life which is creative and mystical. Life after the black despair of the quest—the drouth in the desert of the mystic—the agony in the storm. In some such way is felt the searing of the great light-flash when the spirit breaks forth in daemonic power. Once it was seen as the mighty and four-fold and flashing cherub that Ezekiel told of, and Orpheus called it the Primal Eros bursting in flame from the World-egg which, in the coils of the snake, was blown into vital being by the four winds.

Such is the great Daemon that lives, however faintly, in each and all of us. It is the genius or the antiself, the guardian at the gate and the dragon in the path. It is the shepherd and the guide, the antithetical, the opposite and the revealer. And revelation comes upon the man who finds his accuser within himself, and so, breaking forth from the negative and repetitive, finds affirmation. But Spirit is the soul's equal and if unmated with soul, fails of perception, falling into blind violence.

And yet no transformation comes without this violence, no great change without its torment. So breaks the light upon the prophets. The four winds of the spirit blow upon the dry bones, their voices are heard amid dark thunder clouds. Eternal attributes of the spirit are they, the image of life complete, the four, the Lion, the Bull, the Man, the Eagle—the Eagle that was the serpent. Flame in the dark-ness; Thunders are they in the light. This spirit it is which enlightens our dark, it is that which was slain and is born again. Once, for the Persian, as a bull it brought life into the world, and again as a lamb was its blood shed on the world's foundation, dying that there might be life. To that end the spirit abandoned the other life that it lived, falling to sleep entombed in the body, the mausoleum in which the soul has laid it enwrapped in gravebands. Eros sleeps thus lapped in the dark of Psyche's chamber. But not only enfolded by a dragon does Eros appear when the creative instant comes, but in fire, bearing the thunderbolt.

Every time the spirit is renewed a new creation takes place. For this is the dying into life, the all-changing transmutation; for a sacrifice is made that there may be communion. In man's imagination comes that awaking which has gone on eternally in creation.

In the revelation of this vigil of the Lord's Day, this Sleep of Shadows, in this dying to live, man finds power and coherence in life —in all life. Moreover that which the sacred ceremony of communion sets forth in its traditional symbols—in the bread for body and soul and the wine for spirit and life—that too is part of the same holy and mystical wonder.

Man's hidden interior universe contains the whole great world of images. All there is dark, monstrous and infirm, until the great light of the burning spirit breaks out into life. Then the great ruler appears to give form to all that wild outflow of the ME. The secretive nature mother brings into being her spawn and continually is being overwhelmed and in the way to be destroyed by her pullulating offspring. From their mere outflowing nature in time they are given permanence and form in space; for to the "I"—the Spirit—must they be united if they are to endure and pass through time towards fulfilment and completion. From spirit comes the peculiar life—the particular existence which is enduring, shapely, distinct, separate. Without its force and its power the world is a mass of obsessions, a haunting swarm of half-things dissolving each into each, changing and intermixing monstrously in a fluctuating putrescence. Such a corruption goes draining away into the slobbered mud of a marish waste, slow-heaving as it perishes into nothingness—filth and eternal oblivion.

In truth then spirit reveals the way of escape from the limitations which the learned, the wise, would lay upon the soul, binding it in the laws of its own desires. Revelation came by him who has declared the way of the spirit. To honour him let us glorify ourselves by sending forth once more the reverberating seven-thundered asseveration of the great Jehovah—

I AM